Bank Failures in
the Major Trading Countries
of the World

BANK FAILURES IN THE MAJOR TRADING COUNTRIES OF THE WORLD

Causes and Remedies

Benton E. Gup

Q

QUORUM BOOKS
Westport, Connecticut • London

Library of Congress Cataloging-in-Publication Data

Gup, Benton E.
  Bank failures in the major trading countries of the world : causes
  and remedies / Benton E. Gup.
      p.   cm.
    Includes bibliographical references and index.
    ISBN 1–56720–208–X (alk. paper)
      1. Group of Ten.   2. Bank failures—Europe.   3. Bank failures—
  Japan.   4. Bank failures—United States.   5. Bank failures—Canada.
  I. Title.
  HG3881.5.I58G867   1998
  332.1—dc21   98–4976

British Library Cataloguing in Publication Data is available.

Library of Congress Catalog Card Number: 98–4976
ISBN: 1–56720–208–X

First published in 1998

Quorum Books, 88 Post Road West, Westport, CT 06881
An imprint of Greenwood Publishing Group, Inc.

Printed in the United States of America

The paper used in this book complies with the
Permanent Paper Standard issued by the National
Information Standards Organization (Z39.48–1984).

10 9 8 7 6 5 4 3 2 1

Copyright Acknowledgment

The author and publisher gratefully acknowledge permission to reprint the following
material:

George G. Kaufman, "Bank Failures, Systemic Risk, and Bank Regulation," *Cato Journal*
16, No. 1 (Spring/Summer 1996): 17–45. Reprinted with permission of the Cato Institute,
Washington, D.C.

To Jean, Lincoln, Andrew, and Jeremy

Contents

Tables

Bank Failures in
the Major Trading Countries
of the World

Introduction

Banking problems exist throughout the world. An International Monetary Fund (IMF) study by Lindgren, Garcia, and Saal (1996, Table 2) revealed that during the 1980–spring 1996 period, 133 of the IMF's 181 member countries had experienced significant banking sector problems. This study presents the results of a survey of banking problems and their resolution in the Group of Ten countries since 1980. Actually, the Group of Ten countries, or G-10, now refers to eleven countries: Belgium, Canada, France, Germany, Italy, Japan, Netherlands, Switzerland, Sweden, United Kingdom, and the United States. Switzerland became a full member of the group in 1984.[1] These countries play a key role in global monetary affairs and trade. However, they were not immune from banking problems. Although bank failures in the United States have been examined extensively in the literature, bank failures in the foreign G-10 countries have been overlooked. This book is a first step in filling that void.

Most of the research for this study was conducted while I was a Visiting Scholar at the Office of the Comptroller of the Currency (OCC) in Washington, DC during January–May 1997, where I was assigned to evaluate some, but not all, of the issues presented here. The issues of too-big-to-fail and bank regulation were not part of my assignment.

They were, however, a natural outgrowth of my research at the OCC. One cannot study bank failures without wondering why some institutions are not permitted to fail, and about the effectiveness of bank regulation.

Because of my prior affiliation with the OCC, the usual disclaimer applies. The views expressed here are those of the author and do not necessarily reflect those of the Comptroller of the Currency or the Department of Treasury. Equally important, the information used in preparing this document came from the publicly available sources listed in the Bibliography. In this regard, the librarians at the OCC did an outstanding job in helping me to obtain the information I needed.

The OCC used the survey of bank failures in internal documents and reports, as part of its ongoing studies of domestic and foreign banking systems. In addition, some of the results of the survey were presented in a paper coauthored with Philip Bartholomew at the Annual Meeting of the International Trade and Finance Association, May 21, 1997, in Porto, Portugal, and at the Annual Meeting of Southern Finance Association in Baltimore in November 1997. The title of that paper was "A Survey of Bank Failures, Near Failures, and Significant Incidents in Foreign G-10 Countries since 1980." Dr. Bartholomew is the director of the Bank Research Division at the OCC. Other parts of the book were presented at various seminars.

Some important findings of this study are as follows.

- All of the G-10 countries have had bank (depository or credit institution) failures, and most do so on a regular basis.

- The United States, Canada, Sweden, and Japan have been confronted with large numbers of failures and near failures.

- Most of the failures are due to credit problems. Real estate finance problems stand out as being the primary cause of a large number of failures. None of the institutions that we surveyed failed due to traditional insurance or securities activities, with the exception of derivatives activities or credit activities where some form of securities were involved. Fraud accounted for about 10 percent of the failures. These failures were concentrated in small institutions, but fraud appeared in some of the largest ones too.

- Most of the significant incidents involved derivatives activities.

- The too-big-to-fail doctrine goes beyond banks, and it will continue to be one method of resolution of large failures.

- Finally, the effectiveness of prudential bank regulation is questioned. To a large extent, the effectiveness of prudential bank regulation depends on economic stability.

This study is divided into seven chapters, an appendix, and the Bibliography. Chapter 1 defines key concepts that are used in this book. Terms such as *failure* have different meanings in various countries. Chapters 2 and 3 provide a country-by-country discussion of selected failures, near failures, and significant incidents for which information was available. Chapter 4 reviews the failures, near failures, and significant incidents in the eleven countries, and it reveals some common patterns, and some striking differences in their resolution. Chapter 5 deals with the Too-Big-to-Fail issue from an international perspective. Chapter 6 examines the effectiveness of prudential bank supervision. Chapter 7 is a case study of the crisis in Thailand. Doowoo Nam, my graduate student assistant, coauthored this chapter. Although Thailand is not one of the G-10 countries, this study illustrates how banking problems can occur. The Appendix is an article by George G. Kaufman, "Bank Failures, Systemic Risk, and Bank Regulation." It was first published as a Working Paper by the Federal Reserve Bank of Chicago (January 1996, WP96–1); the version that appears here was published in the *Cato Journal* (1996, Vol. 16, No. 1), and it appears with their permission. All of the references cited or used in the preparation of chapters 1–6 are listed at the end of the book. References for Chapter 7, the case study of Thailand, appear at the end of that chapter.

NOTE

1. The Group of Ten was established in 1962 as an informal group of countries that contribute to the International Monetary Fund's General Agreement to Borrow. For additional information, see the *Yearbook of International Organizations, 1996/1997* (1996).

1

Key Concepts

Well-known economist Anna J. Schwartz has said, "With respect to the terms that a reader encounters in the literature, financial fragility, financial crises, and financial instability are as common as systemic risk, but the terms have different meanings for different writers" (1995, 20). Exactly the same problem exists when we are trying to define bank failures, near failures, significant incidents, and other terms used in this book. Nevertheless, a discussion of these and other terms is necessary to provide a framework for this survey. The major concepts covered in this chapter are:

Contagion

Crisis

Failure and Near Failure

Insolvent

Panics

Resolution

Runs

Significant Incidents
Systemic Risk

CONTAGION AMONG BANKS

According to Gilbert (1988), a contagious bank *panic* occurs when information about troubles at some banks induces depositors to *run* on other banks, even though they have no new information about those banks. Kaufman (1995) defines *contagion* (*systemic risk*) as the probability that cumulative losses will occur from an event that sets in motion a series of *successive* losses along a chain of institutions or markets comprising the system. The spillover in the United States, according to Kaufman (1990), may be due to

1. The large number of depositors.
2. The number of dollar amounts of correspondent balances and Federal funds borrowed from other banks.
3. The presence of foreign deposits.
4. The role that banks play in the payments system.

Kaufman (1990) states that the 1980s experience of banks and savings and loan associations in Texas shows that national contagion or spillover beyond institutions perceived to be in the same boat is highly unlikely.

Although contagion is widely discussed in the literature, recent examples in banks are lacking. Nevertheless, contagion effects also include the impact of bank failures on the share prices of other banks. Swary (1986) found stock market contagion effects from the failure of Continental Illinois bank and First Republic Bank, the two largest bank failures in U.S. history. Madura and Bartunek (1994), Madura and Tucker (1991), Lamy and Thompson (1986), Peavy and Hempel (1988), and Aharony and Swary (1983) found similar results from selected bank failures.

Conglomerates

The term *contagion* is also used in connection with conglomerates, and the possibility that the losses of one activity may reduce the capital available to support other parts of the group. A paper drafted by the Basle Committee stated that it was essential that the parent company of a financial conglomerate and its shareholders should be a source of strength for the other parts of the group (GAO, *International Banking*, 1994, 15).

CRISIS

Banking

Kane (1993) pointed out that the word *crisis* comes from the Greek word for "decision." In business and political situations, a crisis is a policy emergency that calls for the rapid and decisive resolution of what may become an unsustainable situation.

Davis (1995, 354) defines crisis as a major collapse of the financial system, entailing the inability to provide payments or allocate credit.

Kindleberger (1996, 97) states that "a crash is collapse of the prices of assets, or perhaps the failure of an important firm or bank. A panic is a sudden fright without cause, from the god Pan, [which] may occur in asset markets or involve a rush from less liquid to more liquid assets. Financial crises may involve one or both, and in any order."

Friedman and Schwartz (1963) associate banking crises with monetary policy. A banking crisis represents a contraction of the money supply which, in turn, affects aggregate economic activity. Mishkin (1991) argues that asymmetric information plays an important role in banking crises: it may lead depositors to believe that some banks may be *insolvent*. Because they cannot distinguish between high-risk and low-risk banks when there are adverse economic conditions (e.g., asset price deflation), there is a *run* on the banks to obtain cash. He states that the asymmetric information approach complements the monetarist view in that it helps to explain the timing patterns and other features of crises.

Sundararajan and Balino (1991, 3) define a crisis as a situation in which a significant number of financial institutions have liabilities in excess of the market value of their assets, leading to *runs*, and other portfolio shifts, the collapses of some financial firms, and government intervention. Another definition of a crisis is a large number of failures of banks and/or other financial providers, such as thrifts.

Schwartz (1995) states that a financial crisis is based on the fear that payments will not be available at any price, and it is precipitated by the desperate actions of the public to obtain cash, which squeezes the reserves in the banking system. In an attempt to restore reserves, the banks may call loans, refuse to extend credit, or sell assets.

Raymond Goldsmith (Kindleberger, 1996, 3) defines a financial crisis as "a sharp, brief, ultracyclical deterioration of all or most of a group of financial indicators—short-term interest rates, asset (stock, real estate, land) prices, commercial insolvencies and failures of financial institutions."

Kaminsky and Reinhart (1996) define the beginning of a crisis as bank runs leading to the closure, merging, or takeover by the public sector of one or more financial institutions; or if there are no runs, the closure, merging, takeover, or large-scale government assistance of financial institutions. Examples of crises include, but are not limited to, Argentina (1980, 1985, 1994), Denmark (1987), Finland (1991), Indonesia (1992), Israel (1983), Mexico (1992) Norway (1988), Peru (1983), the Philippines (1981), Spain (1977), Sweden (1991), Thailand (1983) Turkey (1991), United States (1982–1993), Uruguay (1982), and Venezuela (1993).

Honohan (1997) observed that many crises are *endemic*, persisting for years and usually traceable to pervasive government involvement. Other crises are *epidemics*, sometimes involving macroeconomic collapses.

The *Financial Times* (January 28, 1997) reported that bank analyst Brian Waterhouse notes that individual banks are in crises when they are unable to obtain funds at any price, and their capital is exhausted and below the 8 percent risk-based capital ratio. Finally, the troubled bank goes to the central bank for help. Schwartz (1995) uses the term *financial distress* to describe individual banks or other firms in trouble.

Causes

The competitive process is at work. Firms earning normal profits on their existing products may all simultaneously be attracted to new products offering growth potential. However, individual firms cannot predict if other firms will enter that market, or if they do, the likelihood for success. Once investments have been made, and there are large sunk costs, some firms may stay in the market, even if there are initial losses. Exiting too early might adversely affect their reputations. Staying in the industry leaves them vulnerable to adverse changes in the financial markets (Davis, 1995, 225).

Eisenbeis (1995) made an extensive review of the literature and found that the research evidence supports the notion that the relationship between financial crises and changes in real economic output runs from the real sector to the financial sector, and not the reverse. There are no examples in the history of the United States, where the economy was running at a high level of output, when a financial crisis resulted in a contraction in the real economy. Moreover, government actions played a significant role in both creating and mitigating the crises.

Goldstein and Turner (1996) attribute international banking crises to:

1. Macroeconomic volatility: external and domestic.
2. Lending booms, asset price collapses and surges in capital inflows.

3. Increasing bank liabilities with large maturity/currency mis-matches.

4. Inadequate preparation for financial liberalism, which, according to Sheng (1996, 30) allows banks to take excessive risks in areas where they have no experience.

5. Heavy government involvement and loose controls on connected lending.

6. Weaknesses in accounting, disclosure, and legal framework.

7. Distorted incentives for owners, managers, depositors, and supervisors

8. Exchange rate regimes.

Davis (1995, 198) found the following features in international financial crises:

1. They followed a shift in the regime that had unknown consequences.

2. There were structural changes in financial markets leading to increased competition.

3. Innovation and declining capital ratios of lenders and borrowers were often important.

4. They often followed periods of monetary tightening.

5. There were sharp increases in price and quantity of credit.

6. Sometimes there was a collapse of liquidity in securities markets.

7. For crises in Euromarkets, international transmission was swift and strong.

8. Contagion between markets was limited.

Davis (1995, 198–99) states that the *preconditions* for a financial crisis are:

1. A long period of calm conditions with intense competition between financial institutions.

2. Increasing and concentrated debt accumulation at low-risk premiums.

3. Financial innovation and declining capital ratios.

The *triggering* of a crisis may occur as a result of:

1. The tightening of monetary policy, and the unknown consequences of a shift in regimes, including the properties of financial innovations.
2. Asset devaluation.

The financial crisis may entail:

1. Runs, panics, asset devaluations that lead to sharp increases in the price and quantity of credit as well as reduction of liquidity in security markets.
2. Intervention by the authorities to prevent contagion and recessions: government intervention prevented the crisis from having systemic and macroeconomic consequences. However, in the case of the savings and loan crisis in the United States the cost was very high.

According to Bartholomew and Whalen (1995a), the factors that contributed to U.S. bank failures were:

1. High interest rates in the late 1970s and early 1980s contributed to national and regional economic problems (e.g., in the Southwest and New England).
2. Concentration of loan portfolios in real estate loans.
3. Commodity price declines.
4. Deregulation of product and geographic markets.
5. Relaxed chartering provisions for banks.
6. Spillover problems from the "thrift crisis."

Sachs et al. (1996) examined the impact of the Mexican peso crisis in 1994 on other countries—the so-called Tequila Effect. They found three factors that determined a country's vulnerability to financial crises: a large appreciation of the real exchange rate, a weak banking system, and low levels of foreign exchange reserves. To paraphrase Darwin, the fittest countries survived—those without large appreciations in real exchange rate, with strong banking systems and ample foreign exchange reserve, did not have crises.

FAILURE AND NEAR FAILURE

There is no precise definition of *failure*. Nevertheless, the term is generally understood to mean that an institution is nonviable, which means that it cannot operate. The term *insolvent*, which is discussed below, is associated with failures.

Failure is a regulatory or legal decision. Accordingly, another definition of failure is that a bank regulator has closed the institution or has resolved it. Resolving it may mean that shareholders and uninsured creditors have lost their investment, and management has been replaced, but the institution continues to operate. This definition is after the fact. Alternatively, one could say that regulatory intervention occurs during the process of failing. If the regulatory intervention is successful, the institution may be restored to a viable state at best, or avoid being liquidated at worst. Therefore, banks that are in the process of being resolved, or have been restored to a viable state, are considered *near failures*. The term *resolution* is discussed below.

Failure is not always an option. Ange and Carreras (1989, 52) asked why no French banks have gone bankrupt? Their answer was that "there is a system of solidarity organized by the French Treasury Department that makes it very difficult for a bank to go bankrupt, even if it wants to." Bankruptcy is the transfer of residual ownership from equity holders to the creditors. It is hard to go bankrupt when the bank is government-owned.

Bank failures are not necessarily bad. Lindgren et al. (1996, 114–115) assert that the exit of weak individual banks is critical for the maintenance of a strong banking system. Moreover, experience has shown that unsound banks are invariably in worse condition than is indicated by their financial statements, and that the lowest-cost way to keep the banking system sound is to force the early exit of unsound banks.

INSOLVENT

Insolvent in a legal sense means that a debtor is unable to pay debts when they are due, regardless of the value of assets and liabilities. In the United Kingdom and some European nations, bankruptcy is referred to as insolvency.

Insolvency also means that the book or market value of a firm's assets are worth less than that of its liabilities. Thus, insolvency is determined by market forces. In this context, *insolvency* is not the same as *nonviable* in a financial sense. As long as the firm has a positive cash flow, it can continue to operate, regardless of the relative value of its assets and liabilities. In the case of leveraged buyouts (LBOs), the firms typically have negative equity.[1] However, banks in this condition are in distress—they are insolvent, but not necessarily illiquid, according to Sundararajan and Balino (1991, 4). This is consistent with the Basle

Committee on Banking Supervision's *Report to the Governors on Supervision of Banks' Foreign Establishments* (1975), known as the Basle Concordat of 1975, which defined solvency as the ability to meet current obligations as they come due.[2]

The European solvency ratio is the ratio of capital (own funds) to on-and-off balance sheet commitments weighted according to their degree of risk. The minimum solvency ratio, or risk-weighted capital ratio as it is called in the United States, is 8 percent. FDICIA (Section 131, Prompt Corrective Action) requires regulators to arrange for an orderly resolution when an institution's capital ratio falls below certain levels— that is, it is insolvent. A bank is considered critically undercapitalized if its risk-weighted capital ratio is 4 percent, or its core capital ratio is less than 2 percent (capital/assets). The bank must be placed in conservatorship or receivership within 90 days.

PANICS

Gorton (1985) states that a panic occurs when there is a sudden shift in the perceived riskiness of demand deposits at all banks, leading to a large-scale transformation of deposits into currency. According to Calomiris and Gorton (1991), a banking panic occurs when "debt holders at all or many banks in the banking system suddenly demand that banks convert their debt claims into cash (at par) to such an extent that the banks suspend convertibility of their debt into cash or, in the case of the United States, act collectively to avoid suspension of convertibility by issuing clearing-house loan certificates."

Gilbert and Wood (1986) state that failure of one bank leads people to fear for the safety of their funds at other banks. Attempts to withdraw funds from those banks may put them in jeopardy. Park (1991) identified the lack of bank-specific information as the principal cause of bank panics.

The last banking panic in the United States was in 1933, the same year that deposit insurance was established. The last panic in the United Kingdom was in 1866, and the Bank of England intervened to prevent disruption of the banking system. Panics may or may not involve *contagion* or *failure*.

RESOLUTION

According to Bartholomew and Whalen (1995a), the U.S. Government Accounting Office defines *resolution* as "taking" an institution, determining its estimated cost of resolution on a present-value basis, and committing to a strategy of liquidation, transfer of insured deposits, or purchase and assumption. This definition is too narrow, because in the United States and elsewhere, resolution of problem banks takes many forms. It ranges from liquidation at one extreme to nationalization at the other end of the spectrum. In between are various methods of resolution, including "bad banks," bank holidays, restructuring, and other techniques that are not addressed here. A bad bank refers to the acquisition of a bank's nonperforming assets by another bank—the bad bank—that was established by the government and/or others for that purpose. Restructuring refers to the sale of assets and downsizing. Political pressure is also used. For example, during the 1987 stock market crash, the Federal Reserve "encouraged major banks to lend to solvent securities firms, coordinated with the Treasury, and encouraged officials to keep the New York Stock Exchange open" (United States General Accounting Office, Bank Oversight, 1996, 31–32). Which techniques will be used and "the timing of an intervention . . . is, and will always remain, a question of judgment" (Canada Deposit Insurance Corporation, *Annual Report 1993*, 4).

RUNS

Bank failures are sometimes associated with runs. The Federal Reserve Bank of Cleveland (1986) defines a run as a loss (net withdrawal) of more than 1 percent of total deposits per banking day that cannot be explained by seasonal or other factors unrelated to depositors' confidence. Gilbert (1988) states that a run occurs when individual depositors suddenly demand currency because of concern about the safety of their deposits. This conventional type of run refers to retail deposits. A run may involve one or more banks. In October 1995, Japan experienced a run on its Hyogo Bank and Kizu Credit Cooperative. The Bank of Japan, Japan's central bank, had to truck in billions of dollars worth of yen in one day to meet the demands of depositors (Nanto, 1995b).

A *silent run* occurs when large financial institutions, foreign banks, or corporations sell their negotiable CDs or the commercial paper of banks that show signs of financial weakness, and in which they have no confidence. This happened to Continental Illinois Bank in 1984.

Some runs may be precipitated by newspaper headlines or television backdrops. On January 4, 1994, "Damaging Loss Expected for the Bank of New England" was a front page headline of the *Boston Globe*. This article helped to shape public opinion and contributed to the run on the Bank of New England. Similarly, Cable News Network (CNN) did a story on bank closings and used a branch of Old Stone Corporation in Rhode Island as a backdrop. Although Old Stone Corporation was solvent, and not in trouble, there was a run on the bank (Lohr, *New York Times*, February 18, 1991, 33).

SIGNIFICANT INCIDENTS

The term *significant incidents*, as used in this book, refers to large and unusual losses incurred by banking or other organizations that may or may not have resulted in failure. Many of the significant incidents reported here are attributable to losses associated with derivatives activities.

SYSTEMIC RISK

A General Accounting Office (GAO) study of international banking (1994c, 19) stated that because of the increasingly global nature of banking, a systemic failure is "the ultimate fear of supervisors." The GAO defines systemic crisis as "a disruption that severely damages the operation of the financial system either within a country or across country borders and, at the extreme, causes the system to break down completely." The concept is extended to take into account real economic activity by Bartholomew and Whalen (1995b), who define it as "the likelihood of a sudden, usually unexpected, collapse of confidence in a significant portion of the banking or financial system with potentially large real economic effects." However, the extent of the adverse effects of such a crisis is unknown. It may be severe, mild, or nonexistent. Gorton (1988) and Tallman (1988) argue that past bank panics may not have caused declines in real economic activity. The panics may be linked to business cycle activity. Wall (1993) points out that there are some unresolved issues when a large bank fails, especially with respect to the disposition of over-the-counter derivatives products such as interest rate, foreign exchange, and commodity swaps. Accordingly, neither legislators nor regulators want to deal with the consequences of what might happen in the future.

The fear of systemic risk was sufficiently important that it was addressed by the U.S. Congress in the Federal Deposit Insurance Corporation Improvement Act of 1991 (FDICIA). If the least-cost resolution of the bank failures would not suffice, the Act (P.L. 105, Sec. 141, G) gave the Secretary of the Treasury (in consultation with the President) and bank regulators the authority to deal with the failure of insured depository institutions that would have "serious adverse effects on economic conditions or financial stability."

NOTES

1. See Samson and Gup (1989) for a discussion of LBOs.
2. The Basle Committee on Banking Supervision was established in 1975 by banking supervisory authorities from the G-10 countries. To-

day it also includes representatives from Luxembourg. Sometimes this group is referred to as the G-10 + 2; referring to the original G-10 countries plus Switzerland and Luxembourg. The Committee usually meets at the Bank for International Settlements in Basle, Switzerland, where their permanent Secretariat is located.

2

Country Analysis I

Because the amount of information available for each country varied widely, the presentations for each country differ in format and content. Bank failures are listed in chronological order. Where possible, background information is given in the introductory comments. Because bank failures in the United States are examined extensively in the literature, only selected failures are presented in this book. This is the first of two chapters containing country analysis. The countries covered in this chapter include: Belgium, Canada, France, Germany, and Italy; the remaining G-10 countries are covered in the next chapter.

BELGIUM

Financial Institutions

Bank failures are not common in Belgium. Banque pour l'Amerique du Sud, which failed in 1976, was the first bank to fail since banking reforms were instituted in Belgium in 1935. This small bank was a subsidiary of an Argentine family-owned group. It failed under "mysterious circumstances." Two other small banks failed in the 1970s; both failures involved fraud (Goodhart, 1995, 374–376).

Banque Andes, 1980

Banque Andes was a medium-size bank that had liquidity problems and it was threatened with a run on deposits. A large portion of the depositors were foreign. The shareholders wanted to dispose of the bank or liquidate it. It was taken over by another bank without loss to the shareholders or depositors.

Geoffrey's Bank, 1980

Poor liquidity, poor management and control procedures, and excess concentration of loans in the problem sector of the economy were the downfall of this medium-size bank. The bank was acquired by Groupe Bancaire Besbanque, a member of a foreign financial group.

Banque Copine, 1982

The Bank Commission insisted on reorganizing this bank because of its financial condition and weak management. Adverse press comments led to a run on the bank's deposits. The government's Rediscount and Guarantee Institute opened a line of credit to the bank and gave it a loan of 500 million francs. The bank was taken over by Famibanque, another bank incorporated in Belgium.

Bank Max Fischer, 1997

Bank Max Fischer was closed in 1997 by Belgian regulators. The two managing partners of the bank were indicted on charges of money laundering. In addition, there were widespread illegal dealings and tax evasion by diamond merchants. Antwerp is a major international diamond center, and Max Fischer was one of the main banks financing the diamond trade (DuBois, July 3, 1997).

Significant Incident

Credit Lyonnais Belgium, 1997

Credit Lyonnais Belgium lost $100 million or more (five times the bank's profit) due to employee fraud. A female employee siphoned funds from foreign exchange and treasury transactions into accounts and companies controlled by her husband. The crime reveals a lack of internal controls (Buckley, 1997).

CANADA

Background

The Canadian economy entered a boom that began in the late 1970s, which led to heavy borrowing by energy and agricultural firms. That

Table 2.1
Financial Institutions, Canada[a]

Institution	Number	Percent of Industry Assets
Schedule I banks	9	84.6%
Schedule II banks (domestic)	2	1.2
Schedule II banks (foreign)	53	7.4
Trusts	20	1.7
Loan companies	10	4.1
Cooperative credit associations	7	0.8
Total	101	100.0%

[a]Data are for October 31, 1994. In Schedule I banks, no shareholder holds more than 10 percent of the bank's voting shares. Schedule II banks are owned by domestic and foreign banks.

Source: United States General Accounting Office, *Bank Regulatory Structure: Canada*, 1995a, 13.

period ended in a recession in 1982, and there were weaknesses in commodity prices in 1985. In the early 1990s, there was a weak market for real estate and other assets, and increasing cost pressures on banks as a result of intensified competition.

Kryzanowski and Roberts (1989) state that because of the small number of large banks, the Canadian government provided an *implicit* guarantee to the public—implicit because it was never put into law— that no chartered bank would be allowed to fail. This guarantee, rather than national branch banking, which provided geographic diversification, was the primary reason that no Canadian banks failed during the depression in the 1930s. An *explicit* guarantee for depositors of chartered banks and federally incorporated trust and mortgage companies was granted with the creation of Canada Deposit Insurance Corporation (CDIC) in 1967. The CDIC insures deposits up to C$60,000 at all member financial institutions except credit unions and certain provincial institutions. The Quebec Deposit Insurance Board insures deposits at all depository institutions except banks in the province of Quebec.

Financial Institutions

Northland Bank and Canadian Commercial Bank (CCB), 1985

In 1985, Northland Bank and CCB, two relatively small Alberta-based banks, were the first chartered banks closed since the liquidation of Home Bank in 1923 (fifty-two years earlier). Northland had problems with real estate and energy loans, and CCB had problems with loans for oil rigs. The banks had funded their growth in the wholesale money market. In March 1985, CCB told the Bank of Canada that the loan loss provision required by bank regulators would exceed their capital. Northland Bank had been receiving liquidity assistance from other banks since 1983.

As problems at both banks became known, a run began on their deposits, and major banks withdrew their money market support. To avoid a loss of confidence in the banking system, the Central Bank, the "Big Six" major banks, and the deposit insurers provided a C$225 million support package. Their fear of loss of confidence was due to the recent Ohio and Maryland thrift crises, problems with S&Ls in the United States, and with Johnson Matthey Bankers in the United Kingdom. All depositors were covered, even beyond the limits of the insurance. The total cost of the rescue was about C$900 million (Davis, 1995, 252; Goodhart, 1995, 376; Jayanti et al., 1996).

Mercantile Bank of Montreal, Continental Bank of Toronto, and Morguard Bank of Vancouver, 1985

Three other banks—Mercantile Bank of Montreal, Continental Bank of Toronto, and Morguard Bank of Vancouver—had financial difficulties and were taken over by larger banks. The three banks experienced a significant loss of deposits because of the lack of depositors' confidence (Binhammer, 1988, 220; Davis, 1995, 252; Goodhart, 1995, 377).

Bank of British Columbia (BBC), 1985–1986

Financial problems at BBC in 1984 resulted in restructuring of the balance sheet and a change of management. In 1996, BBC closed one-third of its domestic branches and its office in London. Additional management changes were announced. BBC was acquired by Hong Kong and Shanghai Banking Corporation, with a payment of C$200 million made to that bank by the CDIC (Goodhart, 1995, 378).

Dominion Trust Company, Prenor Trust Company, and Monarch Trust, 1993–1994

Three CDIC-insured institutions—the Dominion Trust Company, Prenor Trust Company of Canada, and Monarch Trust Company—failed and were liquidated during the January 1, 1993–March 31, 1994 period. Dominion Trust was adversely affected by a downturn in the economy. It had losses on real estate loans, and it was undercapitalized. The bank was liquidated and most of the deposits transferred to other institutions. Prenor Trust Company of Canada had had losses since 1991. Most of its deposits were transferred too. The CIDC paid depositors at Monarch Trust Company C$65 million.

Several other companies ceased taking deposits, or were amalgamated with other institutions. The Royal Trust Corporation, and its affiliates, were purchased by the Royal Bank. The Montreal Trust Company, and its affiliates, were purchased by the Bank of Nova Scotia. Neither transactions resulted in costs to the CDIC (Canada Deposit Insurance Corporation, *CDIC Annual Report 1993*, 2, 10).

Failure Resolutions

Listed in Table 2.2 are the failures and their cost in Canada during 1980–1995. A careful examination of the data reveals that most of the failures were of small financial institutions. This is a pattern that is repeated in other countries, but similar data detailing the number and cost of failures, were not readily available. Although examining the cost of resolution is beyond the scope of this study, the data presented here show that there is a substantial difference between the initial outlays and the amount expected to be recovered.

Most of the failures of small institutions in Canada and elsewhere were not especially noteworthy in a macroeconomic or financial sense, except for the number of them. They do, of course, have local economic effects. As in other industries, the greatest failure rate is among small firms.

FRANCE

There are ninety-nine foreign-owned banks in France. Of that total, eighty-three are headquartered in other European Union (EU) member countries.[1]

Background

Following World War II, there were two periods of nationalization and then privatization, which is going on now. Goldstein and Turner (1996, 18) observed that most state-owned banks were established to allocate credit to particular sectors of the economy, and they are much more likely to be subject to government direction than privately owned banks. Moreover, all too often, the creditworthiness of borrowers does not receive sufficient weight in the credit decision, with the result that state-owned banks are vehicles for extending government aid to ailing industries.

The 1984 Bank Law eliminated the distinction between commercial banks, savings banks, and medium- and long-term credit banks. All banks, securities houses, interbank agents, and financial companies are regulated by the Commission Bancaire (CB) (*Banks under Stress*, 1992, 52).

Table 2.2
Failures, Payments, and Provisions, Canada, 1980–1995

Year	Institution	Payment and/or Cost	Provision after Recoveries
		C$ millions	C$ millions
1980	Astra Trust Company	21	3
1982	District Trust Company	231	15
1983	Amic Mortgage Investment Corp.	28	14
1983	Crown Trust Company	930	5
1983	Fidelity Trust Company	792	354
1983	Greymac Mortgage Corp.	174	103
1983	Greymac Trust Company	240	143
1983	Seaway Mortgage Corp.	120	4
1983	Seaway Trust Company	300	69
1984	Northguard Mortgage Corp.	28	8
1985	Continental Trust Company	113	0
1985	Pioneer Trust Company	201	25
1985	Western Capital Trust Company	77	3
1985	Canadian Commercial Bank	352	184
1985	CCB Mortgage Investment	35	24
1985	London Loan Limited	24	7
1985	Northland Bank	318	107
1986	Bank of B.C.	200	200
1986	Columbia Trust	99	0
1987	Principal Trust	116	0
1990	Settlers Savings & Mortgage Corp.	43	22
1991	Standard Trust Company	1,164	135
1991	Standard Loan Company	157	0
1991	BCCI	22	4
1991	Saskatchewan Trust	64	9
1992	Shoppers Trust	492	18
1992	Central Guarantee Trust Company, Central Guarantee Mortgage Company, (ACC), Toronto-Dominion Bank	1,684	239
1992	First City Trust (North American Trust Co.)	175	0
1993	Dominion Trust Company	431	25
1993	Prenor Trust Company	821	25
1994	Monarch Trust Company	65	5
1995	Income Trust Company	194	NA

Source: Canada Deposit Insurance Corporation, *CDIC Annual Report 1993*, 25; Canada Deposit Insurance Corporation, *CDIC Annual Report 1994–1995*, 41.

Table 2.3
Financial Institutions, France[a]

Institution	Number	Percent of Industry Assets
Commercial banks	425	59.6%
Mutual and cooperative banks	146	16.2
Savings banks	35	5.8
Municipal credit banks	21	0.1
Finance companies	1,015	10.1
Specialized institutions	32	8.2

[a]Data are for December 1993.

Source: United States General Accounting Office, *Bank Regulatory Structure: France*, 1995b.

The combination of boom-and-bust real estate cycles and over-concentration of real estate loans has hurt French banks. In 1991–1995 there was a real estate boom, followed by a recession in 1992–1993 and a real estate depression in 1992–1995. There was low inflation, but high unemployment and a fiscal deficit (Lindgren et al., 1996, 48.) The CB has shown that "failure of credit institutions [is] always attributable to overconcentration of risks, notably credit or liquidity risks." The concentration of risks is a result of shortcomings in internal controls. In addition, French banks tend to specialize in specific industries, which contributes to excess concentration. The problem is exacerbated because French firms tend to rely on only one major bank for all of their banking services (United States General Accounting Office, *Bank Regulatory Structure, France*, 1995b, 33).

Financial Institutions

Al Saudi Banque, S. A. (Al Saudi), 1988

Al Saudi Banque, S. A. (Al Saudi), a small bank, was in financial distress. Many of its depositors were foreigners and foreign banks that were lending funds in the interbank market. The bank recycled petrodollars to Third World debtors, which resulted in poor-quality loans. The French deposit protection system does not cover deposits in foreign currencies or interbank deposits. Section 52 of the 1984 Banking Act gives the BC the authority to "request" assistance in the form of additional capital and/or liquidity when a credit institution is in distress. The assistance can come from the shareholders of the distressed institution and/or other banks. French banks were asked by the Bank of

France to provide over FFr. 1.9 billion to Al Saudi, and creditors of Al Saudi to forgive that debt. Most of Al Saudi's shareholders did not contribute funds to rescue the bank. Only one, Indosuez's Middle Eastern affiliate, the Hariri group of Saudi Arabia, contributed funds, but it was not enough. French banks were aware of Al Saudi's weak condition and would not lend to it in the interbank market. Foreign banks apparently did not know of its condition (Goodhart, 1995, 383; Kyei, 1995).

One of the primary goals of the rescue plan was to protect the reputation of French markets. Foreign depositors and creditors were completely paid off, but French depositors were only partially compensated. Al Saudi's assets were transferred to France's Banque Indosuez, which supplied about 35 percent of the bank's new capital; the Hariri group of Saudi Arabia; and Thomson, a French-owned electronics firm (United States General Accounting Office, *Bank Regulatory Structure, France*, 1995b, 53, 54, 55).

Banque Internationale pour l'Afrique Occidentale (BIAO), 1988

The BIAO was bailed out by Bank Nationale de Paris (BNP), which was under pressure from the CB to provide assistance. The failed bank's capital was restructured, and provisions for sovereign debt were brought up to 40 percent ($101.5 mn), wiping out its capital (Goodhart, 1995, 383).

Kuwait French Bank and BAII, UBAF, 1989–1990

Bank Nationale de Paris, Credit Lyonnais, and CIC, as minor shareholders, were forced by the CB to take over Kuwait French Bank and BAII, UBAF (Goodhart, 1995, 383).

Banque de Participations et de Placements (BPP), 1989

BPP was created in 1985 after the takeover of the former Banque Stern by the Lebanese banking group INTRA. An inspection by the CB revealed falsified loan documents that hid the extent of the bank's loans to INTRA. The CB required new capital to be injected, but the stockholders refused. The bank's license was withdrawn, it was liquidated, and sold to the French Lagarde Group (Goodhart, 1995, 384).

United Banking Corporation (UBC), 1989

UBC, a 100 percent Lebanese-owned bank, failed in 1989 when its license was revoked for fraud in connection with lending to high-risk countries. Most of its deposits were in foreign currency, from nonresidents. The bank was liquidated (Goodhart, 1995, 384).

Lebanese Arab Bank, 1989

This Lebanese-owned bank failed in 1989 and was liquidated. Its nonresident depositors were not covered by the deposit insurance fund (Goodhart, 1995, 384).

Credit Lyonnais, 1993–Present

Credit Lyonnais was incorporated as a private bank in 1863, and it was nationalized in 1946. The French state held 80.7 percent of the shares in 1994. Credit Lyonnais, the country's largest bank, had assets of nearly FFr 2 trillion and employed over 71,000 people worldwide. Its operations included commercial, investment, and merchant banking, third-party funds management, insurance, and other activities ("Commission Decision," 1995).

Under the chairmanship of Jean Yves Haberer (1988–1993), the bank expanded aggressively, almost doubling its assets, extending its retail network across Europe, and it engaged in risky corporate loans and investments that turned sour. According to the "Commission Decision" (1995), Haberer paid "very high prices" to acquire Chase Banque de Commerce in Belgium, Banco Comercial Espanol and Banca Jover in Spain, Creditor Bergamasco and Banca Lombarda in Italy, Bfg in Germany, and Slavenbug Bank in the Netherlands. Examples of failed loans and investments include the Swiss holding company Sasea and loans to the Canadian property group Olympia and York. The Rotterdam subsidiary of the bank loaned money to Italian financiers to buy Metro-Goldwyn-Meyer studios in Hollywood. The bank also invested heavily in real estate. On the liability side of the balance sheet, Haberer had a debt policy that entailed high financing costs. Given the deteriorated quality of the assets and the high cost of liabilities, Credit Lyonnais had losses of FFr 1.8 billion in 1992, FFr 6.9 billion in 1993, and FFr 12 billion in 1994.

The government's recognition of the problem and response to it were slow. The CB said that "it had started to get suspicious in 1991 after seeing Credit Lyonnais's balance sheet increase 30 percent over the previous two years, with a 200 percent rise in industrial holdings" (Buchan and Jack, September 29, 1994). However, the CB did not disclose the problems until the First Rescue Plan in 1993. The problems were not corrected. More financial aid was forthcoming from the government in the Second Rescue Plan plan in 1994. A Third Rescue Plan, costing about $19 billion, was requested in 1995, and an additional $5.26 billion was expected to be added to the rescue plan in early 1997 to help cover the cost of loans being written off, and to improve the bank's solvency ratio.

The first two Rescue Plans were devised so that nothing would appear in the government's budget for the next twenty years. However, that was not the case for the Third Rescue Plan. This time, the bill for the bailout would appear in the budget. Two large French banks (Banque Nationale de Paris and Societe General) complained that the earlier aid package distorted competition.

The Third Rescue Plan was suggested by the bank's Executive Chairman, Jean Peyrelevade. In addition to his position at Credit Lyonnais, Peyrelevade was also the nonexecutive director of Barings Bank. He wants the state to take over the problem loans and assets and separate the good bank from the bad bank. The bad bank is a state-owned entity called the Consortium de Realisation (CDR). The CDR will be backed by a twenty-year loan from Credit Lyonnais. Because of this accounting magic, Credit Lyonnais will rid itself of its troubled assets, which are estimated to be more than $27 billion. These assets include $8.44 billion in commercial real estate, three finance subsidiaries, and industrial holdings that include Metro-Goldwyn-Mayer movie studios. The restructuring plan also called for the elimination of 1,500 workers from a labor force of 38,000. Because of labor laws and unions, the bank has had difficulty in reducing its labor force.

Credit Lyonnais has been downsizing. It sold some or all of its retail operations in Argentina, Brazil, Chile, the Netherlands, Peru, Philippines, and Sweden. Part of the bailout included selling 35 percent of its commercial assets outside France to generate cash. However, while the sale of Bfg in Germany would generate cash, it would also generate a capital loss because it will be sold below acquisition cost. Other asset sales include a book-and-record chain, a life insurance company, a specialist glass firm, a television station, and a hotel chain. While the bank is downsizing, it is also adding new products. Credit Lyonnais is expected to issue American Express cards to employees of its corporate clients. This would break ranks with the national payment card association that operates Visa International and MasterCard International. (Flemming, 1997).

In March 1997, Credit Lyonnais Belgium reported that it lost $100 million, five times the bank's profits, due to employee fraud (Buckley, 1997). Nevertheless, Credit Lyonnais, the French bank group, reported a small profit of $35.6 million (Jack, March 21, 1997, 19). Against this background, the bank's chairman, Jean Peyrelevade, agreed to sell its Dublin-based financial services company, acquired in 1990, which provides auto and equipment leasing. However, he said that he would resign if the European Commission forces him to sell their operations in New York or Tokyo (Jack, March 24, 1997; Jack and Brown, March 14, 1997).

Credit Industriel et Commercial (CIC), Groupe des Assurances Nationales (GAN), 1996–

The government agreed to privatization of selected financial institutions. However, the privatization process did not go well for Credit Industriel et Commercial (CIC), the retail banks that are owned by the Groupe des Assurances Nationales (GAN), a troubled state-owned insurance group. CIC owned a 49 percent share of UIC, a property lender that had huge losses following the decline in real estate values in 1992. There were only two bids for the retail regional banks, from Banque Nationale de Paris and Societe Generale, both far below CIC's book value. If the government cannot sell the insurance activities of GAN and CIC, the estimated cost of the rescue package is more than $3.5 billion (Buchan and Jack, September 29, 1994; "Debit Lyonnais's encore," 1996; Jack, February 22, 1997, March 5, 1997; Jack and Tucker, January 8, 1997; Lindgren et al., 1996; Nash, 1995; "A Sorry Way," 1995; "Taxpayers," 1996; Tucker and Jack, July 27, 1997; United States General Accounting Office, Bank Regulatory Structure, France 1995b, 17, 18).

Credit Foncier de France (CFF) and Suez Group, 1996

Credit Foncier de France (CFF), a bank that specializes in subsidized low-income housing loans, announced large losses of $2.2 billion, which wiped out more than its shareholders' capital. It was saved from bankruptcy because the government granted a line of credit, and the finance minister promised that CFF's bonds would be honored. The bank tried to reduce expenses by cutting the labor force by 1,800 jobs. However, union protests delayed the layoffs. In February 1997, Credit Immobilier was considering buying some of CFF's housing loans, but it wanted to hire only 1,500 of CFF's staff of 3,300 (Credit Immobilier, 1997).

In May 1996, the Suez Group, one of France's largest conglomerates, sold its controlling share of Banque Indosuez, its investment bank, to Credit Agricole, the nation's largest mutual bank ("French Banks," 1996; Jack, March 25, 1997). Credit Agricole is well capitalized, which should help Indosuez's credit rating and reduce its cost of capital.

Both CFF and Indosuez illustrate problems of adjustments to deregulation, which started in the 1980s: CFF's monopoly on supplying subsidized mortgages was broken, which led to hasty diversification. Both CFF and Suez invested in real estate before the market collapsed. Both were also reluctant to restructure.

Table 2.4
Financial Institutions, Germany[a]

Institution	Number	Percent of Industry Assets
Commercial banks	328	28%
Regional giro and cooperative banks	17	24
Cooperatives	2,778	13
Savings banks	704	23
Mortgage banks	33	13
Total	3,860	100%
Foreign subsidiaries and branches	146	5

[a]Data are for December 1993.

Source: United States General Accounting Office, *Bank Regulatory Structure: The Federal Republic of Germany*, 1994a.

GERMANY

Background

German banking is highly concentrated. The three biggest banks in Germany, Deutsche, Dresdner, and Commerzbank, control more than one-third of all commercial bank assets and are the dominant institutions. Banks are allowed to have major equity positions in commercial and manufacturing companies. Deutsche Bank, Germany's largest bank, has equity positions of 10 percent or more in about seventy companies. Deutsche Bank's executives sit on more than 400 corporate boards. Collectively, German Banks own almost 20 percent of the shares of German companies, and they control more than one-third of the voting power of the top ten German companies (Wilmarth, 1992, 1057, 1995, 13).

Although the Herstatt failure occurred prior to 1980, it is included in this survey because of its impact on international banking.

Financial Institutions

Bankhaus I. D. Herstatt, 1974

Herstatt was established in Cologne in 1955. It was a relatively small bank, but it was one of largest dealers in foreign exchange in Germany. The 1973 oil shock increased the volatility of markets and disrupted capital flows. Many banks experienced foreign exchange losses following the unexpected depreciation of some currencies and a tightening of monetary policy in the United States. Franklin National Bank in the United States failed following large losses on foreign exchange trading. Herstatt, Lloyds Bank in Lugano, the Bank of Belgium, and Westdeutsche Landsbank, all had losses. However, Herstatt suffered the most—it failed.

The method of closure caused some controversy. Herstatt's failure was announced at 4:30 P.M., after closure of the settlement system in Germany, which, because of differences in time zones, was at 10:30 A.M. in New York. It defaulted on more than $600 million in claims. It was closed by the German banking authority, and the Bundesbank stopped clearing its account, at a time when Herstatt was heavily engaged in foreign exchange activities. Lepetit (1982) stated that the German authorities wanted to teach speculators and banks dealing with speculators a lesson. West German banks raised a levy to payoff small deposits up to $7,600, but large depositors had to take what the liquidator would give to them, which ranged from 45 percent (West German institutions) to 65 percent (private creditors) of their claims.

The closure had a global impact because of incomplete foreign exchange transactions. It disrupted the operations of the Clearing House International Payments System (CHIPS) and resulted in losses for banks that had irrevocably paid out Deutsche Marks to Herstatt that day. Thus, Herstatt's counterparties were confronted with losses due to the asynchronous settlement of funds. Up to six weeks after the closure of Herstatt, only the strongest European and U.S. money center banks could raise funds at the preexisting interest rate spread. Other banks were charged risk premiums as high as 2 percent, and were virtually excluded from the interbank trading market. (Borio and Ven den Bergh, 1993, 57; Davis, 1995, 154–156, 230; *Bank Regulatory Structure: The Federal Republic of Germany*, 1994a, 19; Goodhart, 1995, 385; United States General Accounting Office).

The Herstatt failure gave rise to the term "cross-currency settlement risk," or "Herstatt risk." It has serious systemic risk implications because foreign exchange transactions account for a large share of the payments in major financial centers, most of which are handled by banks. A key factor giving rise to Herstatt risk is the difference in time zones and operating hours of banking systems across countries. For example, Borio and Ven den Bergh (1993) observed that there is no overlap at all between the operating hours of the large-value interbank transfer systems of the countries with the three most actively traded currencies: the United States, Japan, and Germany.

Schroeder, Muenchmeyer, Hengst and Co. (SMH), 1983

The Schroeder, Muenchmeyer, Hengst and Co. (SMH), a small universal bank, developed serious financial problems as a result of making excessive loans to various affiliated companies in the building machinery group in Luxembourg. It loaned almost eight times its own capital to that group. The Luxembourg affiliates were not required to report to the German bank regulators. When one of the companies failed, the entire group failed. The bankers went to the Bundesbank when they realized that they had a problem. The Bundesbank and the Federal Bank Supervisory Office brought the bank's management and the bank's creditor banks together to deal with the failure. The creditor banks were persuaded to forgive some debts and accept delayed payments on other debts. The creditor banks did this, in part, because they were concerned about their international reputations, and because of pressure from bank regulators. SMH's securities and other profitable businesses were sold to Lloyd's Bank. The remainder of the bank was dissolved (Goodhart, 1995, 385; United States General Accounting Office, *Bank Regulatory Structure: The Federal Republic of Germany*, 1994a, 30, 33–34).

BCCI, 1991

This bank closed two branches.

Significant Incident

Metallgesellschaft, 1993

M.G. Corporation, the U.S. subsidiary of Metallgesellschaft AG, Germany, lost about $1.3 billion trading oil derivatives. M.G. Corporation tried to hedge long-term contracts to supply oil products to retail distributors at fixed prices, with short-term oil futures. When oil prices declined in 1993, M.G. Corporation incurred losses on the hedge, and it had to meet margin calls. While U.S. accounting standards allowed the losses on long position to be offset by unrealized gains on the forward contracts, German accounting practices would not allow the offset. Because of some doubt about the creditworthiness of the counterparties in forward contracts, Metallgesellschaft did not use the gains as collateral for borrowing to satisfy the margin call. The liquidation of M.G. Corporation's contracts resulted in large losses, and debates about their hedge (Folkerts-Landau et al., 1995, 17).

ITALY

Financial Institutions

Banca Steinhauslin, SpA, 1981–1992

After one of the bank's directors was arrested for fraud and misappropriation of funds, another private bank, Credito Romagnolo, provided some of Steinhauslin's liquidity needs. The Banca d'Italia, the central bank and supervisor, appointed three special administrators to run the bank. When operations were returned to normal, the bank was sold to a small private bank (Goodhart, 1995, 390).

Banco Ambrosiano, Vatican Bank (Istituto per le Opere di Religione, IOR), 1982

Roberto Calvi was the president of Banco Ambrosiano, Italy's largest private bank and its largest bank failure with an initial loss estimate of $1.3 billion in 1982. The bank had a unique role as a Roman Catholic bank. Until a few years before it failed, investors had to produce a baptismal certificate to buy shares in the bank. In addition, Banco Ambrosiano had close ties to the Istituto per le Opere di Religione (IOR), or the Vatican Bank as it is commonly called, a state bank of the Vatican. The Vatican Bank's depositors are Catholic religious orders, clergymen—including Pope John Paul II—and Vatican employees. Archbishop Paul Casimir Marcinkus, formerly of Chicago, was named president/chairman of the Vatican Bank in 1971. He joined the board of a Banco Ambrosiano affiliate in the Bahamas. The Vatican bank became a small shareholder in Banco Ambrosiano (1.6 percent) as well as in its Bahama and Luxembourg affiliates. Ultimately, the Vatican bank owned 10 percent of Banco Ambrosiano.

A 1978 report prepared by Bank of Italy Inspectors reported that Suprafin S.p.A had borrowed money from Banco Ambrosiano and, under direction of the bank's officials, used those funds to buy the bank's stock in a series of transactions from 1974 to 1978. Suprafin sold the shares to shell companies in Panama and Liechtenstein. The inspectors reported that Suprafin appears to have been created by the top officials of Banco Ambrosiano, suggesting that Calvi was misusing bank funds. Ambrosiano officials told the inspectors that Suprafin was owned by the Vatican Bank, and provided a letter, signed by the Vatican Bank officials, to support their view. The Inspector's report also listed complex and questionable transactions between the Vatican Bank and companies controlled by Calvi. On October 16, 1979, the Vatican bank received two time deposits worth $134.2 million from Banco Ambrosiano's Peruvian affiliate. Then the Vatican Bank lent that same amount to a Panamanian company, United Trading. Some of the funds were used to buy Banco Ambrosiano's stock. The Vatican Bank owned United Trading. One reason for the stock accumulation is that Calvi was afraid of a hostile takeover of his bank. Stock held by the Vatican Bank was in friendly hands.

In early 1982, directors of Banco Ambrosiano's Peruvian affiliate questioned hundreds of millions of dollars of loans that had been made, under orders from Italy, to a group of Panamanian corporations. At least one-third of the funds were invested in Banco Ambrosiano stock and in other activities. The value of the shares in Italian lire had fallen sharply relative to the dollar-denominated loans used to finance their purchase, resulting in large losses.

Because of the pressure from the Peruvian directors, Calvi asked the Vatican Bank to sign "letters of patronage, to help establish the borrowers' reputation." The September 1, 1981 patronage letters stated that the Vatican Bank directly or indirectly controlled Panamanian and Luxembourg companies, and that it was aware of their debts. In an interview, Archbishop Marcinkus claims that the Vatican Bank did not own any Panamanian companies. However, a letter sent by the Vatican Bank to a Banco Ambrosiano in Luxembourg asks the affiliate to manage the books of several Panamanian companies.

In early June 1982, when Banco Ambrosiano's board of directors voted to cooperate with the Peruvian affiliate and demanded explanations concerning the failed loans, Calvi fled the country. On June 17, 1982, the board of directors of Banco Ambrosiano dissolved itself, stripped the Chairman, Calvi, of his power, and called the Bank of Italy to rescue it.

The next day, Roberto Calvi was found hanged from London's Blackfriars Bridge. It is believed that he was murdered because of his activities with the Mafia. In April 1997, an arrest warrant was served on the "treasurer" of the Cosa Nostra, the umbrella organization for the Sicillian mafia, for alleged involvement in Calvi's death. In July 1981, Calvi had been convicted of violating currency export laws, and he was imprisoned until August of that year. At the time of his death, he was facing fraud charges in connection with stock prices of a company belonging to Michele Sindona, who was serving a twenty-five-year prison term in the United States. Sindona was involved with the failure of Franklin National Bank in 1974, which was the largest bank failure in the United States. Calvi was reported to be a member of the secret, right-wing Masonic Lodge P2, which was assumed to have subversive purposes. Its members included political and military officials in Italy and South America.

The initial losses for Banco Ambrosiano were estimated to be $1.3 billion. However, creditors recovered about 70 percent of their claims, but most of the shareholders lost their investments. The old bank was declared bankrupt, and the Nuovo Banco Ambrosiano was founded with capital from seven banks and with funds from the Bank of Italy, so that the state held 50 percent of the ownership and the remainder was private. The seven banks are Banca Nazionale del Lavoro (state owned), Istituto Mobiliare Italiano (state owned), Istituto Bancario Sao Paolo di Torino (state owned), Banca Agricola Commerciale (private), Credito

Romagnolo (private), Banca Popolare di Milano (private cooperative bank), and Banca San Paolo di Brescia (private) (Blustein, 1982; Colby, 1987; Goodhart, 1995, 390; Graham, April 10, 1997; Macleod, 1982).

In February 1997, the Italian Treasury was urged by the Istituto Ugo La Malfa report to transform the ownership of the central bank by buying the banks and savings banks that own 84.5 percent of it. This would help reinforce the weak asset base of publicly owned banks at a time when privitization is an important issue. The biggest shareholder is Cariplo, Italy's largest savings bank, with a 10.35 percent stake. Cariplo, meanwhile, wants to form a strategic alliance with Banco Ambrosiano Veneto (Ambroveneto). Credit Agricole, a French group, owns 29 percent of Ambroveneto (Betts, 1997; Graham, February 12, 1997).

Casa di Risparmio di Prato, 1988–1991

This savings bank concentrated its financing on the textile industry in the Tuscany region. When the economy turned down, problem loans increased to over 50 percent of the loan portfolio. The Deposit Insurance Protection fund injected capital, and then arranged for the sale of the bank to another regional bank (Goodhart, 1995, 391).

Banco di Napoli, 1996

This state-owned bank lost $2 billion in 1996, and the government announced an emergency rescue plan ("Coping with the Ups and Downs," April 27, 1997; Tucker and Fisher, 2/4/97).

Significant Incident

Banca Nazionale del Lavoro's (BNL) Atlanta, Georgia Agency Office, 1985–1989

BNL, Italy's largest bank, is 96 percent owned by the Italian government. BNL's Atlanta, Georgia agency office was authorized to conduct limited financing for large commercial customers in nine southern states. Nevertheless, it provided about $4 billion in secret loans to finance Iraq. This was done by keeping secret sets of books on separate computers maintained outside the office, and by making false reports to bank's management in New York and Rome. Nevertheless, there was reason to believe that some officials in Rome were aware of the transactions long before BNL Atlanta's managers were sanctioned. BNL Atlanta also hid the transactions from bank regulators in the United States. BNL Atlanta also had close ties to BCCI (Gup, 1995; United States General Accounting Office, *International Banking*, 1994a, 18).

NOTE

1. European Union (EU) countries include Austria, Belgium, Denmark, Finland, France, Germany, Greece, Ireland, Italy, Luxembourg, Netherlands, Portugal, Spain, Sweden, and United Kingdom.

through public sector institutions (United States Department of Treasury, *National Treatment Study, 1994*, 336).

Background

Keiretsus and Stock Values

The Japanese banking system is highly concentrated, and about ten large "city banks" hold nearly one-third of total assets. Six of the city banks also serve as "main banks" in *keiretsus*, which are corporate groups of banks, insurance companies, trading companies, and manufacturing and marketing firms. The various firms are related through cross-holdings of shares and other relationships. Japanese banks are permitted to own up to 5 percent of the shares of other companies, and 45 percent of the value of the shares they hold is considered part of their Tier 2 capital. The keiretsus own about 70 percent of the shares of publicly traded Japanese corporations. Therefore, when stock prices declined 56 percent from their peak values in 1990, banks' capital adequacy suffered. Moreover, the writeoff of their bad loans is financed primarily by the sale of stocks held by the banks.

Real Estate

Japanese bank loans are highly concentrated in real estate. Direct lending for real estate and construction increased from 9.4 percent to 14.9 percent of banks' total assets from 1981 to 1991. Additional real estate loans were made by bank subsidiaries, such as mortgage companies.

It was estimated that the value of land in Tokyo exceeded that of the value of land in California, which is larger than all of Japan, or that the value of land in Japan was worth four times that of land in the United States (Kindleberger, 1996, 104). Real estate values peaked in 1990, following a tightening of monetary policy when the speculative bubble broke. By early 1997, the value of real estate declined 70 to 80 percent from the peak values. The decline in values caused severe debt problems for banks and other lenders. However, housing loan companies continued to make real estate loans after real estate values had peaked.

In February 1997, there were press reports that the government was going to buy land from troubled mortgage lenders. Sueno Kosan construction company failed in January 1997, the single largest bankruptcy since World War II. In March 1997, an advisory panel to the Ministry of Finance (MOF) took the first step in creating a real estate investment trust to deal with the problem. Public funds would be used to buy about 900 properties, with a book value of more than $3 billion, from government agencies that repossessed them from failed lenders. The investment trusts would allow investors to buy and sell portions of the property in small lots. Laws dealing with real estate taxes and securitization were changed to help revive the real estate market (Dawkins, April 1, 1997; Sapsford, March 19, 1997, April 1, 1997).

Monetary Policy Actions

From 1992 to 1996, monetary policy was eased and interest rates were lowered to stimulate economic growth. The low discount rate of 0.5 percent was the lowest in any industrialized country since the 1930s. The steep yield curve contributed to bank profitability, and allowed the banks to write off loans. In addition, the bank of Japan announced that it would provide temporary liquidity to institutions announcing losses due to increasing their provision for loan losses. It also eased some accounting provisions concerning reporting of losses on equities in interim reports.

The strong U.S. dollar in 1997 hurt Japanese banks with loans denominated in dollars. While their loan portfolio is growing, their balance sheets, which are denominated in yen, are suffering. Larger loan portfolios mean the banks need more capital. One estimate is that every time the value of the dollar increases 10 yen, big Japanese banks' reserves, on average, cover 0.4 percent less of those loans (Steiner, 1997).

Financial Institutions

Toho Sogo Bank and Toyo Shinkin Bank, 1992; Cooperative Credit Purchasing Company (CCPC), 1993

In 1992, the Deposit Insurance Corporation (DIC) provided 8 billion yen in funding for Toho Sogo Bank's merger with Iyo Bank, and 20 billion yen for Sanwa Bank for its merger with Toyo Shinkin Bank. Toho Sogo was a provincial bank that had problems when its largest customer, a shipbuilder, ran into financial difficulties. Sogo bank, which provided credit to small and medium-sized firms, was converted into a commercial bank in 1988. Toyo Shinkin Bank, an Osaka-based credit union, had problems with forged certificates of deposits and bad debts (*Banks under Stress*, 1992, 53; Goodhart, 1995, 392; Okina, 1993).

With official estimates on nonperforming loans at $120 billion in 1992, one-third of which were not collateralized, the government announced an $86 billion fiscal stimulation program in August 1992. This included the creation of the Cooperative Credit Purchasing Company, which was established by 162 financial institutions, to buy land from bank portfolios at or below market prices, thereby allowing banks some tax relief on the writeoff of nonperforming loans. There was no secondary market for the loans (Nanto, August 19, 1994; Sheng, 1996, 39).

Table 3.1
Financial Institutions, Japan[a]

Institution	Number	Percent of Industry Assets
City banks, credit banks, long-term trust banks	43	56%
Regional banks	129	31
Shinkin banks (nonprofit cooperatives)	358	13
Total	530	100% (Total assets $7,997 billion)
Foreign subsidiaries and branches	170	NA
Total	700	(Total assets $15,993 billion)
Exchange rate 106.61 yen/$		

Note: The total number of financial institutions, including small, specialized institutions is about 1,130. Some of these are not examined by the BOJ.
[a]Examined by the Bank of Japan, March 31, 1996.

Kamaishi Shinkin Bank, 1993

In 1993, Kamaishi Shinkin Bank was closed and some of its assets were taken by Iwate Bank, which applied for DIC financial support.

Nippon Mortgage, Apollo Leasing, 1994

The real estate situation improved somewhat, but it was far from fully recovered. In 1994, Nippon Mortgage, one of Japan's largest lenders, went bankrupt. Apollo Leasing, a leasing company with real estate investments and $8 billion in loans, faced collapse when Sakura Bank turned down a rescue plan. The problem with mortgage lenders is exacerbated by the fact that they have minimal loan loss reserves. In 1994, their nonperforming loans were estimated to be a half-trillion dollars (Davis, 1995, 288–290; Dawkins, February 3, 1997, April 1, 1997; Nanto, August 19, 1994; Sheng, 1996, 22, 39; Wilmarth, 1992 1065).

Cosmo and Kizu Credit Cooperatives, Hyogo Bank, and Tokyo Kyodo Bank, 1995

Credit cooperatives, or credit unions, are supervised by the authorities in the prefectures, and their supervision has been inadequate (Lindgren et al., 1996, 138). The Ministry of Finance (MOF) applied forbearance to insolvent credit cooperatives from 1993 to 1995, but they did close some of them. The MOF established the Tokyo Kyodo Bank to take over the nonperforming loans of Tokyo Kyowa Credit Cooperative and Anzen Credit Cooperative in March 1995. According to Zang (1995), these two institutions were alleged to have made most of their bad loans to one property company, thereby breaking the Japanese banking law that limits loans to any one borrower to 20 percent of total capital. Various credit cooperatives "donated" money to Tokyo Kyodo Bank.

In essence, Tokyo Kyodo is a *bad bank*, or *lifeboat institution* as it is called in Japan. Tokyo Kyodo bought the nonperforming assets of failed credit cooperatives. The term *convoy system* is used when stronger companies help weaker ones in their collective interest.

Japan experienced runs on its Hyogo Bank and Kizu Credit Cooperative. The Bank of Japan had to truck in billions of dollars' worth of yen in one day to meet the demands ($1.03 billion) of the depositor's runs. Both institutions failed on the same day—July 30, 1995. Hyogo was the largest bank failure in Japan, and it had bad loans of $8.1 billion. Hyogo's operations were sold to other banks, but the BOJ provided temporary funding until the sale was completed.

Kizu was chartered in Osaka as an employee credit union. When real estate prices began to soar in the 1980s, Kizu expanded its deposits from $2.2 billion in 1988 to $12 billion in 1995 by offering high rates on CDs. Kizu invested heavily in real estate. Kizu continued to loan money to borrowers who would not repay their previous loans (Nanto, October 6, 1995). When economic growth stalled in the early 1990s, real estate prices collapsed, and so did Kizu. It had deposits of $12.2 billion and bad loans of $6.1 billion.

The failures of Hyogo and Kizo came two days after the failure of Cosmo Shinyo Kumiai, another Tokyo credit cooperative that also experienced a run and required an emergency loan from the BOJ. Tokyo Kyodo Bank took over the Kizu and Cosmo credit cooperatives, (Andrews, 1995; Nanto, December 17, 1995, October 11, 1996; "Regional Bank," *BNA*, 1995).

In 1995, the Ministry of Finance was coping with about $400 billion in nonperforming loans (Nanto et al., December 19, 1995). Unofficial estimates reach $1 trillion, or 25 percent of gross domestic product (GDP) (Caprio and Klingebiel, 1996). Lindgren et al. (1996, 138) report that foreclosures are difficult in Japan. The authorities lack the power to close a failing bank without the consent of shareholders, or a court order.

Housing Loan Companies (jusen), Housing Loan Administration Corporation (HLAC), 1996

Housing loan companies *(jusen)* are non-deposit-taking subsidiaries of banks that were created to provide affordable home financing for

individual borrowers. Nevertheless, eighteen of the top twenty borrowers were real estate companies located in Tokyo and Osaka. After Japan's real estate bubble had burst, *jusen* continued to make mortgage
loans. Some of them lent money "so indiscriminately, that certain build-
ings are now being occupied by gangsters who not only refuse to make
mortgage payments but stand to gain by driving down the value of the
property and buying it when it comes up for auction. Some jusen borrowers have been arrested" (Nanto, October 11, 1996). Although the
MOF knew of *jusen*'s problem loans as early as 1991, the issues were
not resolved until 1996, when seven out of eight *jusen* failed. The government created the Housing Loan Administration Corporation
(HLAC) to take over the assets of the seven bankrupt companies. It
also acquired bad loans from banks and agricultural cooperatives. The
HLAC is a "bad bank" financed by the government and financial institutions.

The cost of the resolution over the past four years was estimated to
be $19 to $24 billion, of which $7 billion was provided by the Japanese
Insurance Fund. The government appropriated an additional $6.4 bil-
lion in aid to help resolve the $59 billion nonrecoverable loss from seven
housing loan companies. Deposit insurance premiums were increased
(United States General Accounting Office, *Bank Regulatory Structure:
Japan*, 1996b, 2.1).

Hanwa Bank, Kii Bank, Taiheiyo Bank, and Wakashio Bank, 1996–1997

Hanwa Bank, a small regional bank, and several credit cooperatives
failed in November 1996. In April 1997, the MOF announced that a
new caretaker bank, Kii Bank, would be established to take over the
operations of Hanwa. The Bank of Japan provided $79 million in capital
to fund Kii. It is expected that Kii itself will be closed in about five
years (Tett, 1997).

There were depositor runs at some credit cooperatives. Many larger
banks declared losses. The MOF announced that Taiheiyo Bank, a regional bank in Tokyo, would be liquidated. Sakura Bank, and three
other banks that each had a 5 percent stake in Taiheiyo, announced
that they would establish Wakashio Bank to take over the performing
assets of the failed Taiheiyo.

In 1966, the MOF estimated problem loans to be 8 percent of GDP
(Lindgren et al., 1996, 42).

Nippon Credit Bank and Hokkaido Takushoku Bank, 1997

Finance Minister Hiroshi Mitsuzuka stated the MOF's support of the
largest twenty banks remains firmly in place, reflecting Japan's too-

big-to-fail policy. However, stories in the press about Nippon Credit Bank and Hokkaido Takushoku Bank stated that the problems may be too big to resolve. Nippon is the third largest credit bank in Japan, and Hokkaido Takushoku Bank is the smallest of the top ten commercial banks. According to one analyst, John Plender (April 1, 1997), there was "talk in Tokyo for the need for one or more large banks to be allowed to fail, to convince the public there can be no solution to the banking crises . . . without using taxpayer's money." Using the policy of *constructive ambiguity*, which means guarantees for the biggest banks, administrators have had troubled banks solve their own problems by reducing loans, dividends, branches, and staff.

Nippon Credit had not done these things to the extent that it could by early 1997, and it was thought that the government might shut it down. But that did not happen. By late March, the picture for Nippon had changed. Hiroshi Mitsuzuka reiterated that the Bank of Japan (BOJ) would extend credit to help Nippon Credit. First, it will receive additional capital of about $569 million from commercial banks that were asked by the BOJ to join the effort to help Nippon. An additional $1.2 billion of capital will come from life insurance companies, and $700 million from the BOJ of Japan. Its affiliates, Crown Leasing, Nippon Total Finance, and Nippon Shinyo, had total debts of $16.4 billion. They filed for bankruptcy in April. Moreover, Nippon agreed to withdraw from overseas operations, sell key real estate holdings, and reduce employment by 20 percent.

Hokkaido Takushoku Bank agreed to sell or close its overseas operations and merge with Hokkaido Bank, a leading regional lender. Together, they will become a "super regional" bank with total assets of $109 billion when the deal is completed in April 1998. The new combination will be called Shin Hokkaido Bank (Dawkins, April 2, 1997; Dawkins and Robinson, April 2, 1997; Robinson, April 1, 1997; Sapsford, February 11, 1997; "Sayonara," 1997; Sugawara, March 29, 1997).

Significant Incidents

Bank of Credit and Commerce International (BCCI), 1991

The Industrial Bank of Japan deposited 44 billion yen in BCCI's Tokyo branch, for which payment was to be received in New York from BCCI's New York branch. When BCCI was closed in 1991, the dollar portion of the transaction was not completed. Consequently, the Industrial Bank of Japan became a creditor for $30 million. Settlement of foreign exchange transactions originating in the Far East may be delayed in settlement through CHIPS as much as fourteen hours (Eisenbeis, 1995).

Daiwa Bank Ltd., 1990s

Daiwa Bank is Japan's tenth largest bank, and the twenty-fourth largest bank in the world with $176 billion in global assets. Of that total, $11.9 billion was invested in the United States in 1994. The bank's problems were unauthorized trading and lack of internal controls; in addition, it deceived regulators.

The New York branch of Daiwa Bank had $1.1 billion losses resulting from over 30,000 trades covering eleven years of trading U.S. Treasury securities. The loss stemmed from the actions of a rogue trader, Toshihide Iguchi. He apparently covered his losses by selling bonds held in custodial accounts and falsifying records. The bank's managers hid his actions from U.S. bank regulators. In addition, Daiwa Bank Trust Company had lost about $97 million in trades between 1984 and 1987, some of which were unauthorized.

On November 2, 1995, U.S. bank regulators ordered Daiwa to close its operations in the United States by February 2, 1996. The United States District Attorney brought a twenty-four-count criminal indictment against Daiwa. The Japanese bank was fined $340 million. In Japan, the Ministry of Finance penalized the bank's parent company (Greenspan, November 27, 1995; Nanto, December 27, 1995; Nanto et al., December 19, 1995).

The Federal Reserve has an arrangement with the Bank of Japan to provide collateralized loans to Japanese banks facing emergency liquidity needs. This precautionary measure was devised to forestall the sale of large amounts of Treasury securities by Japanese banks in need of funds. Such sales would raise interest rates.

Daiwa Bank Ltd., in the United States, was merged into Sumitomo Bank. This was viewed as "damage control" by the MOF.

Sumitomo Corporation, 1996

Yasuo Hamanaka, the former copper trader at Sumitomo Corporation, one of Japan's biggest trading companies, pleaded guilty to fraud in trading losses of $1.8 billion over a decade. The trading losses depressed world copper prices in 1996 when the fraud was discovered. The trading corporation was a subsidiary of the 300-year-old Sumitomo Bank, one of Japan's largest banks.

Bank of Tokyo–Mitsubishi Bank Ltd., 1997

In March 1997, the New York–based derivatives trading unit of the Bank had a $50 million loss, and costs of $33 million for unwinding its swap portfolio. The losses were blamed on a computer model that overvalued positions. National Westminster Bank PLC (UK) had a $138 million loss earlier in 1997, also blamed on a computer program (McGee, March 28, 1997).

THE NETHERLANDS

Financial Institutions

Amsterdam National Bank (AAB), 1981

AAB was a relatively small subsidiary of Mid-America Credit Corporation. It was involved in trade finance in Latin America. AAB did not comply adequately with instructions from the De Nederlandsche Bank (DNB) to withdraw certain credit facilities from foreign borrowers who were associated with the bank's shareholders. The bank was liquidated. Eligible depositors were paid up to a maximum of 30,00 guilders. Others lost their deposits (Goodhart, 1995, 393).

Tilburgsche Hypotheekbank N.V. (THB), 1981–1983

THB was a mortgage bank that experienced heavy losses stemming from the decline in real estate values. Management was replaced, and three large mortgage banks lent THB 18 million guilders of subordinated debt. However, conditions worsened and THB went bankrupt. While some depositors were covered by the insurance scheme, those with bearer bonds were not compensated. Shareholders also lost their investment (Goodhart, 1995, 394).

Westland/Utrecht Hypotheekbank N.V. (WUH), 1981–1982

WUH was the largest mortgage bank in the Netherlands. It suffered heavy losses due to the slump in the real estate market. Because of rumors about its financial condition, WUH had difficulty raising funds. In 1981, the DNB arranged for four banks and an insurance company to buy WUH. Also, WUH agreed to sell a large portion of its mortgage portfolio to the Dutch state pension fund. Additional funds were provided by the insurance company, Nationale Nederlanden N.V., which acquired a majority interest in WUH. No depositor's funds were lost (Goodhart, 1995, 394).

Friesch-Groningse Hypotheekbank N.V. (FGH), 1982

FGH was the third largest mortgage bank in the Netherlands, and it too was affected adversely by the slump in the real estate market. The Post Office Savings Bank provided both debt and equity funds and took over the bank. No depositor's funds were lost (Goodhart, 1995, 395).

N.V. Slavenburg's Bank, 1981–1983

This bank, which was involved in tax evasion and fraud, had heavy loss provisions. In 1983, Credit Lyonnais took over the bank, which was then called Credit Lyonnais Bank Nederland. Credit Lyonnais guaranteed the loan loss reserves (Goodhart, 1995, 395).

SWEDEN

Background

From 1945 to 1983, the banking structure in Sweden was tightly regulated, and no new banking licenses were granted. Banks were required to hold government bonds, and there were limits on credit and exchange controls. The tight regulations on banks gave rise to specialized financial institutions for housing finance, consumer lending, leasing, and direct finance. These nonbank financial institutions gained market share for financial assets (Davis, 1995, 256). Then the law changed in 1985, and equal capital adequacy rules were applied to all financial institutions. The specialized institutions gradually lost their competitive advantage over commercial banks. In 1991, savings banks were permitted to become limited liability companies (*Banks under Stress*, 1992, 54).

Following liberalization in 1985, there was economic growth and large increases in credit extension. From 1985 to 1990, bank loans for the private sector increased from 46 percent to 60 percent of bank portfolios, while government bonds declined from 25 percent to 11 percent. A number of bank mergers occurred, and there was increased competition for consumer credit and home lending. Competitive pressures were a factor affecting finance companies, which turned to high-risk loans, such as highly leveraged commercial real estate transactions. Banks supplied finance companies with funding in the form of Company Investment Certificates (CIC), which are similar to commercial paper. Lindgren et al. (1996, 139) state that there was insufficient bank supervision, and regulations were lacking on large concentrations of credit to one borrower, and on restraining foreign borrowing.

Capital outflows occurred in 1988–1992. Sweden was in a deep recession in 1992. The exchange rate mechanism (ERM) crises in 1992 led to high short-term rates that hurt banks (Gerlatch and Smets, 1994; Lindgren et al., 1996, 50). Changes in the tax law made real estate investments less attractive, which adversely affected real estate values. When real estate prices declined 50 percent in a short period, and borrowers did not repay their mortgage loans, the finance companies and the banks that financed them were in trouble. Loan losses soared. At the end of 1992, nonperforming loans amounted to 14 percent of the GDP. Almost half of them were real estate related.

The Swedish government and Rikisbank concluded that because Sweden is so heavily dependent on external credit, and because there had been a sharp reduction in the supply of foreign credit, along with pending disaster in the financial sector, they had to restore confidence in its financial sector. Equally important, they had to do it quickly and vigorously. These factors led to the establishment of the Bank Support Authority program, which protected all bank creditors, but not shareholders. There was no upper limit on the degree of protection. This action restored confidence in the banks, and creditors supplied funds without fear of loss. The total cost of the rescue for the banks was estimated to be 4.5 percent of GDP at the end of 1993 (Goodhart, 1995, 400).

Financial Institutions

Nordenbanken, 1991

In 1991, Nordenbanken, which was 80 percent owned by the government and the second largest bank in Sweden, made large provisions for loan losses. Capital was injected, and the government bought back 20 percent of the private sector stock in September 1992. Then Nordenbanken was split into a good bank and a bad bank. The bad bank, Securum AB, was owned by the government, and it took over 60 billion Krona of bad debts from Nordenbanken. The good assets remained at Norden. According to Sheng (1996, 22), the government injected $800 million into the state-controlled Nordenbanken, to guarantee a $609 million loan to save the largest savings bank. The cost of the recapitalization was 6.4 percent of GDP (Caprio and Klingebiel, 1996, 36).

Forsta Sparbank, 1992

In 1992, Forsta Sparbank, a regional savings bank, had large credit losses from loans in the real estate sector. It was rescued with loan guarantees.

Gota Bank, Nyckein Holdings, and Beijer Capital, 1992–1993

Gota Bank, the fourth largest bank, was owned by Gota AB, a Swedish holding company. The holding company applied to the court for receivership; however, Gota Bank was not affected because the Swedish government agreed to guarantee its obligations. The bank was nationalized (Goodhart, 1995, 401).

The highly leveraged Nyckein Holdings and Beijer Capital were unable to roll over their CIC, and the market for such paper dried up. The finance companies sold assets and obtained emergency bank loans. Nevertheless, the banks suffered losses and their capital ratios were on the verge of slipping below 8 percent, a level at which law required the withdrawal of banking permits. Bank closures are subject to the

corporate bankruptcy code rather than being determined by bank regulators (Davis, 1995, 256, 286; Ingves and Lind, 1996).

SWITZERLAND

Background

During the 1980s, the Swiss National Bank, the central bank, allowed the economy to expand rapidly and exports to increase. There
was a large increase in employment: 480,000 people, in an economy of
seven million. As growth and inflation increased, there was increased
investment in real estate. In 1989, the Swiss National Bank changed
its policy and slowed the rate of inflation. Interest rates and the price
of the Swiss franc increased. Another factor boosting the value of the
franc was speculation on the new European currency, the Euro. As the
price of Swiss goods rose, exports declined. Exports account for about
40 percent of GDP. Equally important, real estate values fell. In 1996,
the central banks slashed interest rates to spur economic growth
(Steinmetz, 1997). In 1990, the Banking Act was amended to bring all
nonbank financial institutions under the same regulations as banks,
thereby removing their competitive advantage (*Banks under Stress*,
1992, 54).

Financial Institutions

Weisscredit and Bankag, 1980

These were the largest bank failures in the 1980s. However, they
were small banks. Major banks took over part of their portfolios, and
depositors were given some preference in the liquidation (Goodhart,
1995, 402).

Banque Commerciale SA, 1983

The Federal Banking Commission forced this bank to close because
of its inadequate spread of risks, and because it hid this fact through
its use of a subsidiary in the Cayman Islands. The bank was liquidated
(Goodhart, 1995, 402).

Banca di Partecipazioni ed Investimenti SA (Lugano), Mebco Bank SA (Geneva), Spar and Hypothekenbank AG (Lucerne), 1988–1991

These banks had their licenses withdrawn and were forced into liquidation. Members of the Swiss Bankers Association paid up to 30,000

francs per depositor. This amounts to a *de facto* deposit insurance scheme (Goodhart, 1995, 403).

Caisse d' Epargne du Valais Societe Mutuele, 1987

The Federal Banking Commission persuaded Swiss Banking Corporation to take over this institution. No depositor funds were lost (Goodhart, 1995, 403).

Spar und Leihkasse Thun, 1991

This was a large regional bank that suffered from an overexposure of mortgage credit. The Federal Banking Commission forced the bank to close after three major banks refused to buy it. Their failure to buy the Thun showed that the big banks could not be depended on as the lender of last resort, and that the supervision practices were not adequate. The depositors, however, were protected up to 30,000 francs. The Union of Swiss Regional Banks, which represents about 185 small banks, formed an examination board to examine these banks (Goodhart, 1995, 403).

Bank Ersparniskasse von Konolfingen (EvK), 1992

Bank EvK was one of the largest regional banks that was fundamentally sound. However, it had to make a large provision for bad loans in the previous year, which would result in insufficient capital. It was taken over by Union Bank of Switzerland (UBS) (Goodhart, 1995, 404).

Eko Hypothekar- und Handlesbank, 1992

This large regional bank was closed by the Federal Banking Commission. It was taken over by Credit Suisse, the third largest bank in the country (Goodhart, 1995, 404).

Other Banks

Since 1990, one-third of the banks have disappeared. Most of them were merged into stronger banks. The surviving banks with large reserves have saved the taxpayers from bailing out the weaker banks (Steinmetz, 1997).

UNITED KINGDOM

Background

At the end of 1994, 518 banks were authorized to operate in the United Kingdom. Of that total, 232 were incorporated in the United Kingdom, and 286 were foreign banks. Of the latter, 129 were European-authorized institutions that were approved by their home country supervisors. European-authorized institutions include those in European Union (EU), European Free Trade Area (EFTA), or other nations that participate in the European Economic Area (EEA). In addition, there are eighty-seven building societies that are mutual-deposit-taking institutions specializing in home loans (United States General Accounting Office, *Bank Regulatory Structure: The United Kingdom*, 1994b).

Financial Institutions

Johnson Matthey Bankers (JMB) Limited, 1984

JMB Limited was one of five London gold bullion and commodity traders. A subsidiary of Johnson Matthey PLC, JMB was a relatively small bank, with assets of US$976 million. The bank failure was significant because it was the first one since 1975 in the United Kingdom (Jayanti et al., 1996). When the price of gold declined, the bank turned to commercial lending. The two largest exposures were to two businessmen from Pakistan. These exposures represented 76 percent and 34 percent of the firm's capital. Mahamud Sipra was one of the bank's major clients. Sipra's business was primarily shipping bulk cargo, but he went into the production of films and publishing magazines. Loans to Spira exceeded 10 percent of the bank's capital. Sipra's movies were unsuccessful and he failed. Loans made to others to finance trade in West Africa also failed. The losses on the loans wiped out most of the bank's capital (Goodhart 1995; Ollard and Routledge, 1985).

The Bank of England was aware of the problem at least a year before the bank failed, but did nothing to prevent its collapse. JMB's parent company, Johnson Matthey, PLC, refused to provide enough capital to save the bank. However, it did inject $62 million, and Charter Consolidated PLC injected an additional $31 million. The Bank of England, concerned about London's reputation as a leading international gold bullion market, stepped in to provide support for JMB. The Bank of England persuaded four banks (Barclays, Lloyds, Midland, and National Westminster), as well as members of the gold market and others, to provide £70 million to support JMB. Neither the Bank of England nor any of the other participants experienced any losses from the bailout. The problem had not been recognized or addressed by bank regulators. The result was the passage of the Banking Act of 1987, which dealt with bank regulation and supervision. The Act confirmed the Bank of England's role as a regulator (United States General Accounting Office, *Bank Regulatory Structure: The United Kingdom*, 1994b, 14, 45).

British & Commonwealth Merchant Bank (BCMB), 1990

BCMB was part of a large financial services group (British & Commonwealth Holdings) that had heavy losses in its leasing subsidiary, Atlantic Computers. Some creditor banks refused to renew a standby credit facility to BCMB. Then the firm failed after the Securities Investment Board (SIB) removed BCMB from its list of authorized banks, and it ordered SIB-regulated firms to withdraw their clients' funds. The Bank of England was unable to persuade other banks to provide sufficient credit facilities, and BCMB was closed. Depositors were paid 75 percent of their deposits up to 15,000 pounds (Goodhart, 1995, 406).

Small Banks, 1991

An undisclosed number of small banks failed in 1991 as a result of defaults on real estate loans and consumer credit. The Bank of England provided liquidity to avoid systemic disturbances in the banking system (United States General Accounting Office, *Bank Regulatory Structure: The United Kingdom*, 1994b, 47).

Bank of Commerce and Credit International (BCCI), 1991

BCCI had a complex international structure that allowed it to operate for almost two decades. BCCI's headquarters was a holding company incorporated in Luxembourg. Its main subsidiaries were incorporated in Luxembourg and the Grand Cayman Islands. Neither the holding company nor its subsidiaries did business in Luxembourg. This structure allowed BCCI to move transactions from one subsidiary, in say the United States, and transfer them to another in Hong Kong or Pakistan, thereby shielding their activities from bank regulators and auditors. BCCI had operations in more than seventy countries. Fraud and mismanagement may have caused losses of $5 to $10 billion out of assets of $20 billion (Sheng, 1996, 29). Most of BCCI's business was in England. Illegal loans to the Gulf Group, which was involved in international shipping, amounted to $1.2 billion, of which only $50 million was recovered (Mason, April 4, 1997).

No single banking regulator acted as the lead supervisor over all of BCCI's global activities. Since BCCI's main holding company was located in Luxembourg, the responsibility belonged to the Institut Monteaire de Luxembourg (IML). However, they found it difficult to exercise supervisory control over an organization that had 98 percent of its activities outside its jurisdiction (Gup, 1995; United States General Accounting Office, *International Banking*, 1994c, 17, 38–40).

Significant Incidents

Barings Brothers and Co., Ltd., 1995

Barings was a British bank speculating on Japanese stocks in a Singapore futures market. Its failure involved investors all over the world, and it was acquired by a Dutch banking group. "The one thing that the Barings episode illustrates," said Allan Greenspan, chairman of the Federal Reserve, "is that the productivity for making losses has gone up very significantly in the last 25 years. You couldn't write the execution slips fast enough 25 years ago to lose as much money as was lost by one individual aided by terrific technology," (Hansell, 1995). Barings illustrates the failure of internal controls and the lack of common bank regulation. It also followed other financial derivative incidents involving Orange County, California and Metallgesellschaft's U.S. subsidiary, MG Corporation.

Francis Baring & Co. was established in London in 1762, making it the oldest merchant bank in the United Kingdom. In 1803 it helped finance the Louisiana Purchase. It failed in 1890 because of loans that went bad in Argentina. There was a revolution in Argentina, the President fled the country, and Barings was told that the quarterly payments due on the Republic's bonds would not be paid. Barings faced bankruptcy, but then it was rescued by a consortium led by the Bank of England, which restored it to health. As part of the restoration, the old firm was liquidated, and the new firm was named Barings Brothers and Co., Ltd. (Zang, 1995).

The new Barings built a reputation for financing corporate assets in emerging markets. However, it had little experience in trading for its own account, and that was part of its downfall (Bhalla, 1995). Poor internal controls was another part. Barings' external auditors advised management of deficiencies in internal controls relating to its derivatives activities in 1992, about three years before it failed (Lindgren et al., 1996, 131). There were additional warnings to top management about the trader's activities by his supervisor in 1992, and by an internal audit in 1994 (Bhalla, 1995). The failure to act on such information is gross mismanagement, which includes paying exorbitant bonuses to a trader who than had the incentive to take on more risk.

Barings PLC, the London parent holding company, was bankrupt by a twenty-eight-year-old trader, Nicholas W. Leeson. He joined as a clerk in 1992, and by the beginning of 1994, he was a director and chief trader of Barings Futures Singapore. Leeson, in a twenty-eight-day period, traded stock index futures in Singapore's SIMEX to bet more than $1 billion on the direction of the Nikkei Index of Japanese stocks, and he lost. In doing so, he circumvented the SIMEX's safeguards, and had some control over Barings' back office, which had received $128 million in margin calls (Gargan, 1995). At the end of February 1995, Barings had losses of $1.4 billion versus capital of about $500 million (Bhalla, 1995; Folkerts-Landau and Ito, 1995; Zang, 1995).

Management thought that the Bank of England would come to its aid, as it did in 1890, but that was not to be. The Bank of England argued that taxpayers' money should not be used to cover the losses of speculators. Three divisions of Barings (Baring Asset Management Ltd., which owns a 40 percent stake in Dillion Reed, the New York investment bank, Baring Brothers and Co., and Baring Securities Ltd.) were bought by Internationale Nederlanden Groep (ING), the largest financial service group in the Netherlands. However, they did not acquire the holding company (Barings PLC)

Leeson was arrested, charged with two offenses in Singapore. The first offense was deceiving the auditors of Barings in a way that was "likely to cause harm to their reputation." The second offense was cheating SIMEX. He was sentenced to six and one-half years in prison in Singapore (Leeson and Whitely, 1996, 265).

Barings was a regulated merchant bank trading in a regulated securities market. Additional regulation would not resolve the problem. Barings lacked internal controls and did not have an understanding of risk management in a derivatives age, or the culture to deal with derivatives (Irvine and Shirreff, 1995).

According to Quinn (1996), had information about Barings' futures activities in both Singapore and Osaka been exchanged and subject to a common regulator or to single scrutiny, it is less likely that the bank would have failed.

National Westminster Bank, 1997

National Westminster Bank (NatWest), the United Kingdom's largest bank, reported a loss of about $136 million due to the mispricing of interest rate options on various European currencies. The mispricing was discovered only after one employee had left the bank. Apparently, the mispricing occurred during the 1994–1996 period. The bank stated that their computer models were not at fault. A trader had "aggressively" priced some options, and incorrectly marketed others. An editorial in the *Financial Times* ("Bank Check," 1997) stated that computers cannot substitute for the vigilance of good people. Lack of internal controls dealing with complex options was faulted (Sesit and Calian, 1997).

UNITED STATES

Background

Sheng (1966, 71) states that the United States has the largest banking system in the world. It had about 29,000 deposit-taking institutions at the end of 1991, including 12,500 banks. That was about ten times as many banks per capita as the other countries in the Group of Ten combined. Large numbers result in large numbers of failures. According to a study by Bartholomew and Whalen (1995), during the 1980–1994 period, 1,560 banks were resolved by the FDIC. When adjustments are made for common ownership of holding companies, the total declines to 1,295. During the same period, 1,234 insured thrifts and more than 2,700 credit unions were failed and resolved.

Lindgren et al. (1996, 140) stated that prudential regulation and supervision were seriously deficient, and savings-and-loans (S&L) institutions were allowed to "hide" their insolvency, hoping that their growth would solve their problems. The cost of the thrift crisis was between $315 and $500 billion. The Resolution Trust Corporation acquired $357 billion of bad thrift assets by the end of 1991, and had disposed of $228 billion. The government strengthened the FDIC with $70 million (Sheng, 1996, 22).

Economy

During the 1980–1992 period, the Federal Reserve shifted from targeting interest rates to targeting reserves in October 1979, in order to curtail inflation. The monetary contraction sparked the S&L crisis. Monetary policy was eased in August 1982 in response to the international debt crisis that affected some large banks. It was eased again in the early 1990s, some argue to aid banks, but the easing was also consistent with countering a recession (Lindgren et al., 1996, 50–51, 54, 67).

Interest rate ceilings were phased out (from 1978 to 1982). They became increasingly volatile and reached record levels in the early 1980s. The thrift industry became market value insolvent overnight, and the less developed countries (LDC) debt crisis affected major money center banks. Changes in oil prices contributed to booms and busts. There were recessions in 1980, 1982, and 1990–1992. Commodity price changes (silver in 1980, agriculture in the early to mid-1980s) caused problems for some banks. The exchange rate appreciated until 1986, which hampered exports; then the dollar declined until 1995. Tax reforms in 1986 limited incentives to borrow. Political and tax preferences for housing encouraged overexposure in the real estate industry.

Because bank failures in the United States have been widely discussed in the literature, only selected failures are presented here.

Financial Institutions

Penn Square, 1982

Penn Square Bank was opened in 1960, and was sold to a group headed by Williams Jennings in 1975. At that time the bank had total assets of $33 million. When the bank failed on July 5, 1982, it had over $500 million in assets. Its growth was fueled by selling energy loans. Penn Square Bank sold more than $2 billion in energy loan participations upstream to Continental Illinois ($1 billion); Chase Manhattan ($200–$300 million); Seafirst ($400 million); Michigan National ($190 million); and Northern Trust ($125 million) (Fraser and Richards, 1985; Peavy and Hemple, 1988). Penn Square was not a major bank, but its failure affected other banks because of its distribution of loan participations (spillover effects). Many of the loans defaulted, some because they were fraudulent. The bank had total deposits of about $470 million, of which $220 million were uninsured. The FDIC did not protect the uninsured depositors.

Continental Illinois, 1984

Continental Illinois bank had assets of $41.4 billion when the bank regulators stepped in to rescue it at a cost of over $4 billion. Continental Illinois bank invested heavily in wholesale loans. It had purchased about $1 billion in large participations in high-risk oil loans from Penn Square Bank in Oklahoma. In addition, it had LDC loans. Bad energy and LDC loans were fatal to the bank.

Because Continental could not have branch banks, it depended heavily on uninsured deposits, a large portion of which was held by large institutions around the world. The dollar size of such deposits typically was tens or hundreds of millions of dollars. The institutional investors had a "silent run" on deposits in response to rumors of Continental's problems. The withdrawals reached $8 billion per day, far exceeding the bank's ability to meet them (Davis, 1995, 251; Fraser and Richards, 1985; Jackson, 1995; Wall and Peterson, 1990; Wilmarth, 1992, 988).

According to Kaufman (1990), more than 2,000 correspondent banks had deposits and/or federal funds loans at Continental. Of that total, 200 had balances greater than half their net worth. The Treasury Department (*Modernizing the Financial System*, 1991, 4) puts the number of banks with deposits at Continental at about 1,000. Of that total, 66 had deposits in excess of their capital, and 113 had deposits equaling 50 percent to 100 percent of their capital. Whichever set of numbers is correct, there were large potential spillover effects, and the bank was declared too-large-to-fail when it became insolvent.

Fearing that the failure of Continental would cause systemic risk, the bank regulators planned a rescue for the bank. Part of their fear was due to the fact that the Latin American debt crisis was occurring at the same time, and there were rumors that Manufacturers Hanover might be adversely affected. A $5.5 billion line of credit was provided by twenty-eight banks. The FDIC and a group of banks injected $2 billion of new capital, and the Federal Reserve provided $4.5 billion at its discount window. Finally, the government placed a board member on Continental's board of directors. Some might consider this a weak form of nationalization.

It is argued that nationwide banking could improve safety and soundness through diversification and better information about local conditions. One could argue that both banks would have been better off if they had been allowed to branch into Oklahoma and Texas to obtain better information. However, many banks headquartered in Oklahoma and Texas failed, even though they did have such access.

During the stock market crash in 1987, Continental's First Options of Chicago securities unit had severe losses that were covered by the national bank (Jackson, 1995).

Ohio Thrift Crisis, 1985

The failure of EMS Government Securities Inc., a government securities dealer located in Fort Lauderdale, Florida, on March 4, 1985 created problems for a Cincinnati, Ohio thrift institution. Home State Savings Bank of Cincinnati faced a loss of $145 million because of its dealings with EMS. That amount exceeded Home Savings' capital, plus the total $130 million of deposit insurance assets of the Ohio Deposit Guarantee Fund (ODGF), which insured seventy Ohio institutions. Bank runs ensued at Home State, and at some other ODGF-insured institutions. Governor Richard F. Celeste proclaimed a mandatory closing of all ODGF-insured institutions for five days (March 15–19). On the night of March 19–20, the Ohio legislature agreed to provide assistance, if needed, and required the institutions to convert to federal deposit insurance. Ripples from the Ohio crisis affected Maryland, where there was a run, Massachusetts, North Carolina, and Pennsylvania, which had private insurance funds. Officials in those states then required federal insurance for their institutions (*Federal Reserve Bank of Cleveland Annual Report 1985*).

First Republic Bank Corporation of Texas, 1988

Federal banking regulators allowed two troubled institutions, RepublicBank of Texas and InterFirst Corp., to merge in 1987. First RepublicBank Corporation was the largest bank in Texas, with $32.9 billion in assets when it was closed in July 1988. The idea was that cost savings might keep the two from failing. However, InterFirst's losses were greater than expected, and those combined with Republic's losses resulted in the combined bank's failure.

First RepublicBank was an example of a "bridge bank." Under the Competitive Bank Equality Act of 1987, the FDIC was granted the authority to operate failed institutions for up to three years. Bridge banks are a type of conservatorship, or nationalization. Most of Rebublic-Bank's assets were acquired by North Carolina National Bank (NCNB). The FDIC provided financial assistance by granting a $1 billion loan and $960 million for an 80 percent, nonvoting stake in the firm. NCNB got an option to buy the FDIC's shares at 107 percent of book value over the next five years (Goodhart, 1995, 408; Gordon and Lutton, 1994, 56; United States Treasury, *Modernizing the Financial System*, 1991, 1–33; Wilmarth, 1992, 989).

Freedom National Bank, 1990

Freedom was a small community bank located in Harlem, New York, where many of its depositors were black. When it failed, the FDIC liquidated the bank, but did not completely protect large depositors. Accounts of $100,000 or more were paid $0.50 for each dollar of deposits over that amount. This led to charges of racial bias.

Bank of New England (BNE) 1991

Walter J. Connolly (1991), former chairman of the BNE, said that "the Bank of New England was created specifically in 1985 in response to the changes overtaking the American banking industry. It was the first superregional bank, created by the merging of two leading banks in Connecticut and Massachusetts that traced their roots back to colonial times; and it was run by an experienced group of bankers who shared the bedrock populist belief that the region would best be served if the decisions about its credit were made close to home. A New England Bank for New Englanders, positioned to survive in an increasingly hazardous environment."

Bank regulators publicly acknowledged that the BNE had problems in December 1989. At that time the bank had assets of about $32 billion. Some of the assets were sold to improve the bank's liquidity and to cut its losses. On January 6, 1991, the BNE, with assets of $22 billion, was declared insolvent, and it was taken over by bank regulators, in a bridge bank. Then it was acquired by Kohlberg, Kravis, and Roberts (KKR), and the Fleet/Norstar Financial Group.

The insolvency included the holding company and two subsidiaries: Connecticut Bank and Trust, and Maine National Bank. This was the third largest bank failure in U.S. history, following Continental Illinois ($33.6 billion) and First Republic Bancorp of Texas ($32.7 billion). Weak economic conditions and faulty loans led to BNE's demise.

There were massive deposit withdrawals (runs) on banks in Boston and Providence following the collapse of the Rhode Island Insurance fund in early January 1991. The run on the BNE was estimated to be $1 billion in two days. The depositors redeposited their funds in other large and small banks in New England. For the FDIC, shoring up the economy and protecting depositors were of paramount importance ("For FDIC," *American Banker*, January 8, 1991).

Significant Incidents

Citicorp, 1982

The oil shock of 1979, tight money policies in the United States aimed at fighting inflation, and the appreciation of the dollar all had a negative impact on the growth prospects for developing countries. In August 1982, Mexico announced that it was unable to repay its debts as scheduled. In February 1987, Brazil announced a moratorium on its sovereign debt. In May 1987, Citicorp announced a $3 billion allocation to its loan loss reserves to cover potential losses from loans to LDC. Following this action, about twenty other banks increased their loan loss reserves for LDC debt. Chase increased its reserves by $1.6 billion (Musumeci and Sinkey, 1988). Although Citicorp did not fail, it was in financial difficulty. In late 1991, it had a lower capital ratio and a higher level of nonperforming loans and loan chargeoffs than all but four of the top fifty banks (Meehan and Weber, 1992). According to the popular press, the LDC lending substantially damaged the banks making such loans. Not so, said Logue and Rivoli (1992), reality differed from the press's perception. The banks were wounded, but not really hurting. The high-risk loans were indexed to London Interbank Offer Rate (LIBOR) at rates that compensated them for the risk they took.

Orange County, California, Procter & Gamble, and Gibson Greeting Cards, Inc., 1994–

An Orange County official used floating rate repurchase agreements to leverage the county's assets, and to speculate on interest rates. The official had leveraged the county's assets from $7.5 billion to $20 billion.

He bet wrong, and when interest rates increased in 1994, the county lost $1.5 billion. Orange County went bankrupt when dealers refused to roll over the repurchase agreements (Folkerts-Landau and Ito, 1995, 17).

Orange County is significant because it was one of a series of large-scale losses involving derivatives trading activities that occurred about the same time, when interest rates rose sharply.

Other domestic incidents included Procter & Gamble and Gibson Greeting Cards, Inc. In each case, those who lost billions of dollars claimed to have been duped by greedy derivatives dealers. After an investigation by the Securities and Exchange Commission and the Commodities Futures Trading Commission, Bankers Trust Securities, the securities division of Bankers Trust, was fined $10 million in December 1994, although they neither admitted nor denied the charges that they had violated antifraud laws in the sale of derivatives to Gibson Greeting Cards (Knight, December 23, 1994).

4

Summary of Failures and Near Failures, Resolutions, and Significant Incidents

Details of bank failures, near failures, and significant incidents were presented in the previous chapters. This chapter summarizes the data, revealing some interesting patterns; it is divided into three parts: Failures and Near Failures, Resolutions, and Significant Incidents. In order to avoid repetition, but at the same time glean the important insights, selected summary data are presented in tabular form.

FAILURES AND NEAR FAILURES

Table 4.1 provides a summary of the foreign bank failures and near failures that were examined in this survey. The banks are divided into small, medium, and large sizes. What constitutes small, medium, or large is a matter of judgment based on interpretation of available data. What is large in one country may be medium size in another. With this in mind, the data reveal that most failures were small banks. As noted previously in the survey, many small bank failures were not reported because they lacked macroeconomic or financial significance, except for their numbers. Nevertheless, the data do suggest that small banks are more vulnerable to failure than large banks. When they do fail, they

Table 4.1
Summary of Bank Failures and Near Failures

Name	Year	Nation	Size	Cause of Failure	Resolution
Banque Andes	1980	Belgium	Medium	Lack of liquidity	Acquired
Geoffrey's Bank	1980	Belgium	Medium	Poor management	Acquired
Banque Copine	1982	Belgium	Medium	Poor management	Acquired
Bank Max Fischer	1997	Belgium	Small	Fraud/money laundering	Closed
Northland Bank	1985	Canada	Small	Real estate and energy loans	Capital injection
CCB	1985	Canada	Small	Energy loans	Capital Injection
Mercantile	1985	Canada	Small	Lack of confidence by depositors	Acquired
Continental Bank of Toronto	1985	Canada	Small	Lack of confidence by depositors	Acquired
Morguard	1985	Canada	Small	Lack of confidence by depositors	Acquired
BBC	1985-6	Canada	Small	Financial and management problems	Acquired
Dominion Trust	1993-4	Canada	Small	Real estate losses	Acquired, liquidated
Prenor Trust	1993-4	Canada	Small	Real estate losses	Acquired, liquidated

are less likely to be rescued by the state than large banks. More will be said about this shortly.

The cause of most bank failures is loans that went bad. Within that broad category, real estate loans stand out because they have contributed to more bank failures than any other loan category. In this regard, macroeconomic policies have contributed to boom-and-bust cycles in Japan, the United States, and elsewhere that resulted in asset value deflation and ultimately in loan losses. Sheng (1996, 15) states: "The deterioration of bank portfolios and their rescue by central banks or the state have large monetary and fiscal implications because of feedback effects that lead to a vicious cycle of macroeconomic instability." Thus, macroeconomic shocks, combined with concentrations of real es-

Monarch Trust	1993-4	Canada	Small	Real estate losses	Acquired, liquidated
Al Saudi	1988	France	Medium	Problem loans	Some deposits paid off, assets transferred
BAIO	1988	France	Small	Problem loans	Acquired by state owned bank
Kuwait	1989-90	France	Small	Problem loans	Acquired by bank's shareholder
BAII	1989-90	France	Small	Problem loans	Acquired by bank's shareholder
UBAF	1989-90	France	Small	Problem loans	Acquired by bank's shareholder
BPP	1989	France	Small	Fraud	Liquidated
UBC	1989	France	Small	Fraud	Liquidated
Lebanese Arab	1989	France	Small	Unknown	Liquidated
Credit Lyonnais	1993-	France	Large, Govt. owned	Problem loans	Restructure, capital injections/bad bank/state funds
CIC,GAN	1996	France	Large, Govt. owned	Real estate losses	Privatize, government aid
CFF	1996	France	Large	Real estate losses	Restructure
SuezGroup	1996	France	Large	Real estate losses	Restructure
Herstatt	1974	Germ.	Small	Foreign exchange	Closed
SMH	1983	Germ.	Small	Loans to industrial	Parts acquired,

continued

				affiliate	liquidated
Banca Steinhauslin	1982	Italy	Small	Fraud	Acquired
Banco Ambrosiano, Vatican Bank	1982	Italy	Large	Fraud	State and private capitalization of new bank
Casa di Risparmio	1988	Italy	Medium	Problem loans	Acquired
Banco di Napoli	1996	Italy	Large, government-owned	Losses	Government rescue plan
Toho Sogo	1992	Japan	Medium	Problem loans	Acquired
Toyo Shinkin	1992	Japan	Medium	Fraud	Acquired
Kamaishi Shinkin	1993	Japan	Small	Unknown	Closed
Nippon Mortgage	1994	Japan	Large	Real estate loans	Unknown
Apollo Leasing	1994	Japan	Large	Real estate loans	Unknown
Cosmo	1995	Japan	Large	Problem loans	Bad bank
Kizu	1995	Japan	Large	Problem loans	Bad bank
Hyogo	1995	Japan	Large	Problem loans	Bad bank
Hanwa	1996	Japan	Small	Problem loans	Liquidated, good assets acquired by caretaker bank
Kii	1996	Japan	Small	Problem loans	Liquidated, good assets acquired by caretaker bank

Taiheiyo	1996	Japan	Small	Problem loans	Liquidated, good assets acquired by caretaker bank
Nippon Credit	1997	Japan	Large	Problem loans	Restructure, capital injection from other banks
Hokkaido	1997	Japan	Large	Problem loans	Restructure, capital injection from other banks
Takushoku	1997	Japan	Large	Problem loans	Restructure, capital injection from other banks
AAB	1981	Nether.	Small	Foreign trade finance	Liquidated
THB	1981	Nether.	Medium	Real estate loans	Unknown
WUH	1981	Nether.	Large	Real estate loans	Acquired by private banks/ govt.
FGH	1982	Nether.	Large	Real estate loans	Acquired
Slavenburg	1981-3	Nether.	Small	Fraud	Acquired
Nordenbanken	1991	Sweden	Large, Govt. owned	Unknown	Bad bank, govt. capital injection
Forsta Sparbank	1992	Sweden	Medium	Unknown	Govt. loan guarantees
Gota Bank	1992	Sweden	Large	Unknown	Nationalized
Nyckein Holdings	1992	Sweden	Large	Unknown	Nationalized
Beijer Capital	1992	Sweden	Large	Unknown	Nationalized
Weisscredit	1980	Switz.	Small	Unknown	Liquidated

continued

Banque Commercial	1983	Switz.	Small	Excess risk	Liquidated
Partecipazioni	1988	Switz.	Small	Unknown	Liquidated
Mebco	1988	Switz.	Small	Unknown	Liquidated
Spar	1988	Switz.	Small	Unknown	Liquidated
Hypothhekenbank	1988	Switz.	Small	Unknown	Liquidated
Caisse d' Epargne	1987	Switz.	Small	Unknown	Acquired
Spar und Leihkasse, Thun	1991	Switz.	Large regional	Unknown	Liquidated
Bank Ersparniskasse	1992	Swit.	Large regional	Loan loss provisions excessive	Acquired
JMB	1984	UK	Small	Loan quality/ concentration	Capital support from other banks
BCMB	1990	UK	Small	Loan losses	Liquidated
BCCI	1991	UK and 70 others	Large	Fraud	Liquidated
Penn Square	1982	USA	Small	Fraud/energy loans	Liquidated
Continental Ill.	1984	USA	Large	Problem loans/ concentration	Credit and capital from banks, FDIC
Ohio Thrift Crises	1985	USA	Small	Securities losses	Bank holiday, state assistance
First Republic	1988	USA	Large	Real estate loans, other loans	Bridge bank, acquired
Freedom Bank	1990	USA	Small	Unknown	Liquidated
BNE	1991	USA	Large	Problem loans	Bridge bank, acquired

tate loans, caused our most severe banking crises in the G-10 countries and elsewhere. For example, boom-and-bust economic policies and a real estate bubble that burst were the causes of the 1997 banking crisis in Thailand.

The Basle Committee on Banking Supervision's *Core Principles for Effective Banking Supervision* (1997) recognized the importance of macroeconomic policies. Their preconditions for effective banking supervision state that "providing sound and sustainable macroeconomic policies [is] not within the competence of banking supervisors. Supervisors, however, will need to react if they perceive that existing policies are undermining the safety and soundness of the banking system. In the absence of sound macro-economic policies, banking supervisors will be faced with a virtually impossible task." Even if governments attempt to have stable macroeconomic policies, external factors over which they have no control can raise havoc with banks. The impact of oil shocks and speculative attacks on currency, such as occurred in the European exchange market in the early 1990s, are two examples.[1]

Fraud also played a role in the failure of a significant number of large and small banks. BCCI is the most notable case of fraud on a massive scale, because of its size and the fact that it operated in seventy countries for almost a decade before it was closed. Banco Ambrosiano, Italy, illustrates how one individual, Roberto Calvi, the chairman of a large private bank, with the aid and consent of both insiders and outsiders, manipulated the bank's operations for fraudulent purposes. Calvi was found hanged from a London bridge, allegedly murdered by the Mafia.

Most frauds are less dramatic. They usually involve smaller banks where the owners have a great control over the banks' activities. Most frauds take time to develop, but they are rarely detected before they have done significant harm. Not all large-scale frauds result in failures. Some are reported as the significant incidents that will be discussed shortly.

Finally, a surprisingly large number of the failed banks had foreign ownership, or a large number of foreign depositors. Most of them are small banks located in France, and fraud was a factor in the failures. BCCI was the largest foreign-owned bank that was closed in the United Kingdom and elsewhere.

RESOLUTIONS

The last column in Table 4.1 shows the resolution of the bank failures. In very general terms, the data suggest that small and medium-size bank failures are resolved by liquidation or the banks are acquired by other banks. Large bank failures are frequently resolved by restructuring, which means downsizing by selling off assets and reducing the number of employees. In addition, the larger the bank, the more likely it is that the government will provide capital, acquire nonperforming loans (bad bank), facilitate acquisitions (bridge bank), and use other techniques to minimize the disruption of the failure on macroeconomic activity and the payments system.

The extent of government ownership of a bank is an important factor in determining the resolutions. Large banks that are government-owned will receive government support. Credit Lyonnais is one example. In connection with government-owned banks, the Basle Committee on Banking Supervision's *Core Principles for Effective Banking Supervision* (1997) noted that "correction of problems at these banks is sometimes deferred and the government is not always in a position to recapitalize the bank when required. At the same time, this support may lead to the taking of excessive risks by bank management."

The process of failure and resolution can take many years. It takes time for loan quality to deteriorate, time for the regulators to recognize the problem and to act on it, and time to resolve it. One of the favored methods of resolution is waiting. Regulators combine waiting with other temporary solutions, hoping that macroeconomic conditions will improve enough to save the distressed banks.

SIGNIFICANT INCIDENTS

The data presented in Table 4.2 summarize the significant incidents. Most of the incidents involve large losses associated with derivatives activities. Derivatives, such as swaps, futures, and options, are tools that when used properly are beneficial. Most banks and nonfinancial firms used them for hedging—the transferring of price risks. However, when derivatives are used improperly, they can contribute to large financial losses. Rogue traders working for banks or their affiliates were involved in three of the incidents. In the case of Barings, the bank failed. Daiwa and Sumitomo were strong enough to withstand the losses. The Orange County, California incident involved a local government official who bankrupted the county with his improper trading activities.

These incidents demonstrate a lack of internal controls and knowledge by those who are in positions of responsibility. The trader at Sumitomo had been conducting fraudulent activities for eleven years before large losses brought them to the surface to the extent they could no longer be ignored. Even when such controls exist, the pricing of complex derivatives resulted in losses for the Bank of Tokyo-Mitsubishi and NatWest.

In the corporate sector, Metallgesellschaft experienced losses while hedging long-term contracts with short-term futures in a thin market.

Table 4.2
Summary of Significant Incidents

Name/Year/Country	Cause
Credit Lyonnais Belgium/1997/ Belgium	Fraud by employee, $100 million, five times bank's profit
Metallgesellschaft/1993/Germany, USA	Derivatives, U.S. affiliate hedged, could not cover margin calls. Lost $1.3 billion
BNL-Atlanta/1985–89/Italy, USA	The U.S. agency of an Italian bank made $4 billion in loans to Iraq, exceeding their authority, and made false reports to U.S. regulators
BCCI/1991/Japan	The Industrial Bank of Japan made a deposit in BCCI's Tokyo branch, for payment to be received in New York. BCCI was closed, and the Industrial Bank experienced Herstatt risk for $30 million
Daiwa Bank/1990s/Japan	Derivatives losses of $1.1 billion by rogue trader
Sumitomo Bank/1996/Japan	Futures trading losses of $1.8 billion by rogue trader
Bank of Tokyo–Mitsubishi Bank/ 1997/Japan	Derivatives losses of $88 million, due to mispricing by computer model
Barings/1995/UK	Derivatives losses by rogue trader, $1.4 billion
National Westminister/1997/UK	Derivatives losses of $136 million, due to mispricing by trader
Citicorp et al./1982/USA	Loan losses from less developed countries, reserves for losses were increased
Orange County et al./1994/USA	Derivatives losses of $1.5 billion by county official

This is generally considered a bad idea, although the firm does have some reputable academics on its side, arguing that what they did was correct. Correct or not, they lost a lot of money. In addition to Metallgesellschaft's losses, there were multibillion-dollar losses at Procter & Gamble and Gibson Greeting Cards involving derivatives. It is important to keep in mind that derivatives, per se, were not the cause of the losses. It was their improper use that caused the losses.

Fraud played an important role in three incidents: Credit Lyonnais Belgium, BNL Atlanta, and BCCI.

Finally, Citicorp and other banks involved in lending in less developed countries (LDCs) in the early 1980s were granted regulatory relief by bank regulators as they waited for the debt markets to improve. In the case of the LDC loans, the banks took risks that ultimately paid off. However, the payoff of those loans took longer than expected and it involved government intervention.

NOTE

1. The impact of oil shocks on the economy was a major factor affecting banks in the U.S. Southwest in the 1980s. For a discussion of speculative currency attacks in Europe, 1992–1993, see Gerlach and Smets (1994).

5

Too-Big-to-Fail: An International Perspective

THE DOCTRINE

Banks

The "too-big-to-fail" (TBTF) doctrine received widespread public attention in 1984 when U.S. bank regulators intervened in the case of Continental Illinois Bank because they feared that its failure might cause a systemic crisis. Comptroller of the Currency Todd Conover announced in congressional testimony that the government would not let the eleven largest banks fail. As applied to banks in the United States, the TBTF doctrine means that the organization may continue to exist, and insured depositors will be protected; but stockholders, subordinated debt holders, managers, and some general creditors may suffer losses.[1]

Continental Illinois had assets of $41 billion, and it held the deposits and federal funds of more than 2,000 correspondent banks. Of that total, 200 had balances greater than their net worth (Kaufman, 1990). William Seidman, chairman of the FDIC at that time, said, "Nobody really knows what might happen if a major bank were allowed to default, and the opportunity to find out is not one likely to be appealing to those in authority or to the public" (Dale, 1992, 10).

The main concern with banks is that their widespread failure could lead to a drastic reduction in the money supply with disastrous effects on economic activity (Friedman and Schwartz, 1965, 56; Schwartz, 1988b, 39). First, monetary authorities rely on financial institutions to serve as an effective mechanism for the transmission of monetary policy by changing the quantity of loans made (Bernanke and Blinder, 1992). Second, bank failures also raise the cost of credit intermediation and reduce aggregate demand (Bernanke, 1983; Diamond and Dybvig, 1983). Third, banks play a crucial role in the payments and settlement systems for the payment of goods and services, securities transfers, foreign exchange, and other international capital flows. The collapse of Herstatt bank (Bankhaus I. D. Herstatt) in July 1974 sent shock waves throughout the financial community. There was widespread concern about a breakdown of the payments, clearance, or settlement systems, and governments reacted to protect those systems.

The deregulation and the globalization of world financial markets facilitated the circumvention of domestic credit restrictions, and it has blurred the distinction between banks and other financial institutions (*Banks under Stress*, 1992, 36). In emerging economies, banks bear the brunt of interest rate increases necessary to defend a currency. Therefore, issues of solvency and liquidity in the banking system "quickly move to the top of the agenda in countries experiencing financial distress" (Folkerts-Laundau and Ito, 1995, 8). As increasing numbers of emerging countries are integrated into global capital markets, they will become more vulnerable to external developments, such as cycle changes in industrial countries and shocks in major markets. The 1987 stock market crash and the Mexican peso crisis of December 1994 demonstrate how disturbances in one market may spread to others (Folkerts-Laundau and Ito, 1995, 26).

Because of these concerns about the banking system's central role in the economy, Lindgren et al. (1996, 8) state that virtually no government will permit widespread bank failures, or forbear from intervening to support depositors in the event of systemic bank failures. The size of bank failures is relative. In Hungary, for example, the government put up $67 million as a guarantee against possible losses at Postabank, the country's second largest retail bank, following a depositor run where they withdrew twice that amount. Government officials said that because of its extensive branch network, Postabank was "too important to be allowed to fail" (Lieven, April 25, 1997). However, failure is not always an option. Ange and Carreras (1989, 52) asked why no French banks have gone bankrupt? Their answer was: "Because there is a system of solidarity organized by the French Treasury Department that makes it very difficult for a bank to go bankrupt, even if it wants to."

Beyond Banks

A key point is that the TBTF doctrine goes beyond banks, and it predates the failure of Continental Illinois. Throughout the world, governments intervene in the economy when they *believe* that there is a high probability that any event, for example the failure of a large firm such as Hanbo Steel in Korea, will result in severe economic distress, which they want to avoid. The event may or may not include a systemic crisis. Alternatively, they will enact the TBTF doctrine when they believe that it is in their national interest to do so.

In 1979, the Italian government enacted the Amministrazione Straordinaria Grandi Imprese (D.L. 30.1.1979, n. 26), a TBTF law that deals exclusively with very large nonfinancial firms. In that same year, Chrysler Corporation, the fourteenth largest firm in the United States, almost went bankrupt. The automaker came to Washington for aid, which it received in the form of the Chrysler Corporation Loan Guarantee Act of 1979. The Act provided up to $1.5 billion in federal guarantees to Chrysler through 1983. Total aid, including state and local government funds, suppliers, and deferrals of pension contributions, exceeded $2 billion. By 1984, Chrysler had regained its financial health (Proxmire, 1980; United States Congress, *Findings of the Chrysler Corporation*, 1980; Ross, 1981; Reich and Donahue, 1985).

In the remainder of this chapter, additional nonbank examples of the TBTF doctrine are cited. These examples include government-sponsored enterprises, steel companies, real estate lenders, and commodity traders.

Government Intervention

Government intervention in distressed major industries is not a new concept, nor is it limited to the United States. In the 1930s, for example, the Reconstruction Finance Corporation loaned troubled railroads more than $337 million. Railroads were considered blue chip investments, and their securities were widely held by banks, savings banks, and insurance companies. Thus, the railroads were tied to banks. Ten of the fifteen railroads failed, and railroad bonds became frozen, unmarketable assets for thousands of banks (Olson, 1988, 23).

In the 1980s, the government bailed out a troubled government-sponsored enterprise (GSE). These are quasi-private organizations that have the implied guarantee of the U.S. government. Consider the Farm Credit System (FCS), which lost $4.6 billion. The losses were due to interest rate risk, and to unsafe and unsound lending practices. When interest rates soared in the late 1970s, the FCS funded short-term loans with long-term borrowing. In 1981, the FCS offered farm borrowers loans at 500 basis points below rates offered by competing lenders. When the agricultural economy went into recession, and the speculative bubble on farmland had burst, the FCS announced that it could not meet its obligations without government aid. Congress established a $4 billion program, the Financial Assistance Corporation, to deal with the problem. Because of the implied government guarantee, Standard and Poor's rated FCS obligations as AAA (Ely and Vanderhoff, 1990; Statton, 1989).

In January 1997, when Hanbo Steel of South Korea went bankrupt, the central bank of Korea provided $7 billion of emergency funds to support the company's creditor banks because the government feared that the major banks would fail (Burton, January 29, 1997). Hanbo's debts equal about 60 percent of the bank's capital.

In March 1997 the government of Thailand announced that it would take on the bad debts of finance companies that had overextended themselves in the country's troubled real estate sector. About 10 percent of bank loans and 25 percent of finance company loans are to real estate developers, and half of those loans are nonperforming (Bardacke, March 11, March 12, 1997).

In April 1997, the Japanese Ministry of Finance announced a series of measures to help support its real estate market. Property values declined 70 percent over the last six years, and the Japanese banks and other financial institutions holding real estate were in deep trouble. The rescue package included tax payer's funds to buy property from government agencies that had been repossessed from failed lenders, establishment of real estate investment trusts to encourage the sale of such property, and changes in laws dealing with taxes and securitization (Dawkins, April 1, 1997, Sapsford, April 1, 1997).

Government intervention in the failure of a large firm cannot be taken for granted. Consider the failure of Drexel, Burnham Lambert Group, Inc. in 1990. Drexel was known for selling junk bonds to savings-and-loans institutions that later failed. The holding company wanted to tap $500 million of the capital of its broker-dealer subsidiary, Drexel Burnham Government Securities, Inc. The subsidiary was a primary market dealer for U.S. government securities. When it was clear that federal bank regulators would not pressure banks to lend to the holding company, Drexel, Burnham Lambert Group, Inc. filed for chapter 11 bankruptcy. The failure of Drexel was important because of the interdependence of the payments, clearing, and settlement systems, which are only as strong as their weakest link. However, the government did not intervene in this case (Layne, February 26, 1990; Trigaux, February 16, 1990).

In summary, government intervention appears to be on a selective basis. A detailed examination of the basis for the intervention is beyond the scope of this book. Nevertheless, we can examine the methods governments use to intervene. The following section lists various methods of intervention used in France, Japan, Korea, Sweden, the United Kingdom, and the United States.

METHODS OF INTERVENTION

The Canada Deposit Insurance Corporation *Annual Report* for 1993 (4) states that "the timing of an intervention . . . is, and will always remain, a question of judgement." It goes on to say that "regulatory intervention is the equivalent of the partial or full expropriation of private property, depending upon the severity of the intervention. . . . The policies and procedures for such action need to be spelled out and known in order to maintain both the reality and perception of fairness."

Government intervention can take many different forms depending on its purpose. One purpose is to aid the distressed organization. Another purpose is to reduce the cost of resolution. In this section, twenty-three methods of intervention are examined with examples from a variety of countries. The methods are listed in alphabetical order, except when they are grouped together because of their logical connection.

Assessability, Double Liability, and Source-of-Strength Doctrine

United States

Prior to the passage of the Banking Act of 1933 and national and state banking laws in the United States, the comptroller of the currency or a state bank regulator could assess shareholders of banks to provide additional capital up to the par value of the shares. Successive assessments could be, and were, made, thereby making the shareholders' exposure unlimited. In City National Bank vs. Fuller (52 F.2d. 870, 871, 8th Cir., 1931) shareholders were assessed three times. Those who refused to pay the assessment could have their shares sold by the bank's board of directors. Thus, immediate liquidation of impaired banks, before the situation got worse, was an option available to shareholders (Garten, 1994, 434–435).

Federal law and some states provided for double liability (or greater) for shareholders of failed banks. Congress ended double liability for national bank shares issued after June 16, 1933. However, the double-liability provisions that appeared in 12 U.S.C., 63–64 were repealed in 1959. Colorado law provided for triple liability and California made shareholders liable for all bank debts. The state laws have been repealed.

The fact that the Banking Act of 1933, which created deposit insurance, also eliminated double liability for national bank shares suggests that deposit insurance was considered a better source of depositor protection than the shareholders. Further evidence is the dismal collection rate from shareholders of national banks, which was frequently as low as 50 percent (Garten, 1994, 438).

Since 1972 the Federal Reserve's source-of-strength doctrine has provided that distressed bank affiliates in a holding company can turn to the parent company as a source of financial and managerial strength.[2] The bank holding company can raise funds in the capital markets and downstream those funds to an affiliate bank. This funding option is not available to independent banks in distress. Equally important, the responsibility of a holding company to provide capital for a distressed subsidiary is unique to banking. The source-of-strength doctrine became law in the Financial Institutions Reform Act of 1989 (FIRREA), which requires all commonly controlled banks to be liable for the losses of affiliated banks. However, in this case it is the resources of the affiliated banks, rather than the holding company, that are put at risk. Nevertheless, the holding companies must guarantee the capital restoration plans filed by their undercapitalized affiliated banks (*Building Better Banks*, 1996, 27).

France

Al Saudi Banque, S.A. (Al Saudi), a small bank, was in financial distress in 1988. Many of its depositors were foreigners and foreign banks that were lending funds in the interbank market. The bank recycled petrodollars to Third World debtors, which resulted in poor-quality loans. The French deposit protection system does not cover deposits in foreign currencies or interbank deposits. Section 52 of the 1984 Banking Act gives the BC (the central bank) the authority to "request" assistance in the form of additional capital and/or liquidity when a credit institution is in distress. The assistance can come from the shareholders of the distressed institution and/or other banks. French banks were asked by the Bank of France to provide over FFr. 1.9 billion to Al Saudi, and creditors of Al Saudi were asked to forgive that debt. Most of Al Saudi's shareholders did not contribute funds to rescue the bank. Only one, Indosuez's Middle Eastern affiliate, the Hariri group of Saudi Arabia, injected funds, but it was not enough. French banks were aware of Al Saudi's weak condition and would not lend to it in the interbank market. Foreign banks apparently did not know of its condition (Goodhart, 1995, 383; Kyei, 1995).

One of the primary goals of the rescue plan was to protect the reputation of French markets. Foreign depositors and creditors were completely paid off, but French depositors were only partially compensated. Al Saudi's assets were transferred to France's Banque Indosuez, which supplied about 35 percent of the bank's new capital; the Hariri group of Saudi Arabia; and Thomson, a French-owned electronics firm (United States General Accounting Office, *Bank Regulatory Structure: France*, 1995b, 53, 54, 55)

Bad Banks

The nonperforming assets of a distressed institution can be removed from that institution and taken over by another organization—a bad bank—established for that purpose. The bad bank can be owned by other institutions and/or the government. Examples of bad banks are discussed in the sections on forbearance and nationalization.

Bridge Banks

United States

Under the Competitive Equality Banking Act of 1987, the FDIC was granted the power to establish a "bridge bank" as a temporary means for handling very large bank failures that pose a risk to the stability of the insurance fund. The bridge bank is a federally chartered institution, owned and operated by the FDIC for a period of up to three years. This is another form of conservatorship. The insolvent bank is merged into the bridge bank through a purchase and assumption (P&A) transaction. The bridge bank continues operations until the bank is sold.

The first bridge bank was used to resolve Capital Bank & Trust in Louisiana in 1987. One of the most notable uses of a bridge bank was for the resolution of First Republic Bank Corporation of Texas in 1988. Most of its assets were acquired by North Carolina National Bank (NCNB). First RepublicBank Corporation was the largest bank in Texas, with $32.9 billion in assets when it was closed in July 1988. The FDIC provided financial assistance by granting a $1 billion loan and $960 million for an 80 percent, nonvoting stake in the firm. NCNB got an option to buy the FDIC's shares at 107 percent of book value over the next five years.

Another major resolution using a bridge bank was MCorp, which had about $15.8 billion in assets when it was closed in March 1989. MCorp was acquired by BancOne, an Ohio-based Bank Holding Company (*Failed Bank Cost Analysis*, 1991; Goodhart, 1995, 408; Gordon and Lutton, 1994, 56; United States Department of Treasury, *Modernizing the Financial System*, 1991, 1–33; Wilmarth, 1992, 989).

Delay

United States

In February 1997, President Clinton ordered a sixty-day cooling-off period for a labor strike at American Airlines because he believed that the strike could cause significant economic harm to the economy. A contract between the pilots and the airlines was signed on May 4, ending the strike against the nation's second largest airline (Swoboda, May 6, 1997; Swoboda and Evans, February 15, 1997). The legal basis for the intervention was the 1926 National Railway Labor Act. This Act, intended to deal with national monopolies, grants the President authority to delay strikes that may profoundly affect the economy. American Airlines dominated many airline routes.

Later, in the United Parcel Service (UPS) strike by the Teamsters Union in August 1997, the President could not intervene because it was covered by the 1947 Taft-Hartley Act, which has a higher standard for intervention. The higher standard is a "national emergency." If the President believes that such an emergency exists, then he or she can appoint a board of inquiry. If the board agrees with the President, the Attorney General may seek an eighty-day court injunction.

Deposit Insurance Transfer

United States

The insured and secured deposits of a closed bank can be transferred to another bank that acts as an agent for the FDIC and assumes the responsibility of the payoff.

Depositor Preference

United States

Title III of the Omnibus Budge Reconciliation Act of 1993 contains a provision that revised the priority of claims on failed depository institutions, making depositor liabilities come ahead of general and senior claims.[3] While this law may or may not reduce the cost of resolution for the FDIC, it makes it less attractive for holders of general and senior liabilities to press for bankruptcy. Nondeposit claims get nothing until all depositor claims, including the FDIC as insurer, have been made whole (Helfer, December 11, 1996; Osterberg and Thomson, 1997). Recently, Gary Stern, president of the Federal Reserve Bank of Minneapolis, suggested that uninsured depositors lose up to 20 percent of their deposits above $100,000 if a bank fails (Anason, September 2, 1997).

Forbearance

According to the U.S. Treasury (1991, 1–37) forbearance refers to (1) not enforcing capital or other supervisory standards in financial institutions that are financially troubled, but are judged to be "viable"; and (2) instances in which the FDIC has an ownership position. Therefore, forbearance is not a failure resolution method because it involves institutions that are supposedly financially viable.

Japan

The term *forbearance*, as used here, means waiting instead of closing a financial institution. However, it does not preclude taking various actions. For example, the Japanese Ministry of Finance (MOF) forbearance policy calls for 1) accelerated disposal of nonperforming loans, 2) transferring restructured loans, 3) providing liquidity, and 4) promoting management efficiency (Nanto, 1995a). In 1992, the MOF created the Cooperative Credit Purchasing Corporation (CCCP) to deal with credit cooperatives' problem loans that had real estate as collateral. The CCPC was modeled after the Resolution Trust Corporation (RTC) in the United States. The RTC was a liquidation agency established to absorb the nonperforming assets of thrift institutions that did not meet regulatory capital standards. The cost to the public to contain the savings-and-loan problem was about $215 billion.

Japanese credit cooperatives, or credit unions, are supervised by the authorities in the prefectures, and supervision was inadequate (Lindgren et al., 1996, 138). The MOF applied forbearance to insolvent credit cooperatives from 1993 to 1995, but they did close some of them. The MOF established the Tokyo Kyodo Bank to take over the nonperforming loans of Tokyo Kyowa Credit Cooperative and Anzen Credit Cooperative in March 1995. According to Zang (1995), these two institutions were alleged to have made most of their bad loans to one property company, thereby breaking the Japanese banking law that limits loans to any one borrower to 20 percent of total capital. Various credit cooperatives "donated" money to Tokyo Kyodo Bank. In essence, Tokyo Kyodo is a *bad bank*, or *lifeboat institution* as it is called in Japan. Tokyo Kyodo bought the nonperforming assets of failed credit cooperatives. The term *convoy method* is used when stronger companies help weaker ones in their collective interest. The convoy method is not limited to banks. When Nissan Mutual Life Insurance Company failed in April 1997, the convoy included life insurance companies (Glain and Shirouzu, April 28, 1997).

In 1996, the Japanese Housing Loan Administration Corporation was created to liquidate seven housing loan companies (*jusen*). Four banks formed Wakashio Bank to take over the performing loans of the failed Taiheiyo Bank. In each of these cases, funding was provided by government entities and bank "contributions."

France

In July 1997, estimated losses for Credit Lyonnais for a decade of reckless and fraudulent lending ranged from $17 billion to $30 billion. The Third Rescue Plan for Credit Lyonnais was suggested by the bank's executive chairman, Jean Peyrelevade. In addition to his position at Credit Lyonnais, Peyrelevade was also the nonexecutive director of Barings Bank. He wants the state, and ultimately the taxpayers, to take over the problem loans and assets, and separate the good bank from the bad bank. The bad bank is a state-owned entity called the Consortium de Realisation (CDR). The CDR will be backed by a twenty-year loan from Credit Lyonnais at below-market rates. Because of accounting magic, Credit Lyonnais will rid itself of its troubled assets, estimated to be more than $27 billion. These assets include $8.44 billion in commercial real estate, three finance subsidiaries, and industrial holdings such as Metro-Goldwyn-Mayer movie studios. The restructuring plan also called for the elimination of 1,500 workers from a labor force of 38,000. Because of labor laws and unions, the bank has had difficulty reducing its labor force (Jack and Brown, March 14, 1997; Jack, March 24, 1997).

United States

The Garn-St. Germain Act of 1982 provided for the issuance of *net worth certificates* to qualifying institutions to supplement their capital. These certificates resulted in the creation of "regulatory capital," which forestalled the enforcement of normal capital standards. The first use was for FDIC-insured mutual savings banks in New York and other northeastern states that were having problems due to high and rising interest rates in the early 1980s. Between 1982 and 1986, 29 banks participated in the program, and 22 of them survived. In 1986, the program was applied to 303 banks that were lending in the troubled agricultural and energy sectors. Of that total, 201 survived intact, 35 merged without FDIC assistance, and 67 failed (Hanc, 1996).

The Competitive Equality Banking Act of 1987 contained provisions that allowed agricultural banks to amortize losses from the sale or re-appraisals of qualified agricultural loans and related properties. The unamortized portion of the losses could be included in the primary capital for purposes of regulatory and surpervisory reporting (United States Department of Treasury, 1991, 1, 37–38).

Holidays and State Aid

United States: 1933

When Franklin Roosevelt took office in March 1933, the nation's banks were already closed due to declaration of a bank holiday by the forty-eight states. The term *holiday* was used because the public expects banks to be closed on selected holidays. The purpose of the holidays was to stop bank runs and to restore confidence in the banking system. The presidential declaration of a nationwide, federal bank holiday continued the status quo.

United States: 1986

The Ohio thrift crisis began on March 5, 1986, with the failure of EMS Government Securities Inc., a government securities dealer located in Fort Lauderdale, Florida. Home State Savings Bank of Cincinnati, Ohio faced a loss of $145 million because of its dealings with EMS. That amount exceeded Home Savings' capital, plus the total $130 million of deposit insurance assets of the Ohio Deposit Guarantee Fund (ODGF), which insured seventy Ohio institutions. Bank runs ensued at Home State, and at some other ODGF institutions. Governor Richard F. Celeste proclaimed a mandatory closing of all ODGF-insured institutions for five days (March 15–19). On the night of March 19–20, the Ohio legislature agreed to provide assistance, if needed, and required the institutions to convert to federal deposit insurance. When some institutions were allowed to open on March 20, the dollar amount of monthly withdrawals was limited. Home State's depositors did not have access to their funds until June 14. Home State, and some other ODGF-insured institutions were acquired by other banking organizations from in-state and out-of-state.

Ripples from the Ohio crisis affected Maryland, where there was a run, Massachusetts, North Carolina, and Pennsylvania, which had private insurance funds. Officials in those states then required federal insurance for their institutions (FRB Cleveland, 1986).

The lesson learned from the Ohio thrift crisis is that prompt, effective responses to public concerns are necessary to contain a crisis of confidence in the banking system. Prompt, effective response requires accurate information, understanding the extent of the problem, and the willingness and ability to commit resources to assure depositors protection from loss (FRB Cleveland, 1986).

Liquidation

Liquidation refers to the sale of a firm's dismantled assets. According to Haugen and Senbet (1978), liquidation occurs when the market value of the dismantled assets exceeds the firm's value as a going concern.[4]

United States

Liquidation occurs under chapter 7 of the Bankruptcy Code. In a receivership, the FDIC retains most to all of the failed banks assets to be liquidated (*Failed Bank Cost Analysis*, 1991).

The FDIC's decision to liquidate or to use a purchase and assumption depends on the outcome of a "cost test." Under Section 13(c) of the Federal Deposit Insurance Act of 1950, the assistance provided by the FDIC must not exceed the cost of a payoff and liquidation of a failed or failing institution. The FDIC is not required to select the least costly nonpayoff method. It is only required to estimate the cost (United States General Accounting Office, 1991b, 29).

Liquidity

United States: RFC

In January 1932, Congress passed the Reconstruction Finance Corporation Act, which created the Reconstruction Finance Corporation (RFC) to make secured loans to banks in order to provide them with liquidity to keep them in operation as going concerns. However, loans secured by bank assets actually reduced bank liquidity, and total loans made to nonbank customers declined until 1935. Instead of making loans, banks tended to invest in low-risk government securities.

Bank of America was the first bank to receive a loan. At that time, it was in the midst of a proxy fight for control of the bank. Bank of America received $15 million. In addition, the RFC provided capital to large New York banks and thousands of small, rural banks. Despite RFC backing, the bank runs continued.

In 1933, Congress granted the RFC the authority to provide equity capital in the form of preferred stock to troubled banks. The preferred stock was given equal voting rights with common stock, and it was not subject to assessment to restore impaired capital. The initial dividend on the preferred stock was 5 percent, but it was later reduced to 3 percent. If two dividends were missed, the RFC's voting power was doubled. This made RTC capital more expensive than deposits, because no interest was paid on demand deposits and the rate paid on other deposits was limited by ceilings that could be imposed under the Banking Act of 1933. It was also more costly in terms of corporate governance.

The RFC was considered a temporary response to the banking crisis that was going on at that time. The Act creating the RFC was repealed in 1947. Nevertheless, as late as 1951, the RFC held about $93 million in investments in 392 banks. The RFC was not liquidated until the Reconstruction Finance Corporation Liquidation Act of 1953 was passed (Garten, 1994).

United States: The Penn Central Bankruptcy

In May 1970, Penn Central Railroad was on the verge of bankruptcy and it requested federal assistance from the Nixon administration. Penn Central was a major issuer of commercial paper, with more than $200 million outstanding. Commercial paper was considered almost risk-free because it was only issued by creditworthy corporations. Congress, after lengthy debate, was unwilling to bail out Penn Central. Nor would the Federal Reserve Bank of New York, which had received a request from the Nixon administration to provide a direct loan to the firm. Penn Central declared bankruptcy on Sunday, June 21, 1970.

Recognizing the effects that Penn Central's bankruptcy might have on the commercial paper market, the Federal Reserve Bank of New York encouraged various money center banks to lend to their customers who were unable to roll over commercial paper. The Federal Reserve Bank kept the discount window open to make loans to the banks, and they borrowed $575 million. On June 22, Regulation Q interest rate ceilings on deposits of $100,000 or more were suspended by the Federal Reserve Bank to keep short-term interest rates from rising. The next day the Federal Home Loan Bank Board and the Federal Deposit Insurance Corporation took similar actions. Accordingly, the Federal Reserve Bank acted as a lender of last resort and provided liquidity and influenced the level of short-term interest rates in order to allow the commercial paper market to function (Mishkin, 1991, 98–99).

United States: The Stock Market Crash, October 19, 1987

Monday, October 19, 1987 is called "Black Monday," because the Dow Jones industrial average declined almost 23 percent on a record volume of 604 million shares. This was the largest one-day decline in stock prices on record. The following day, brokers needed to extend massive amounts of credit to their customers who had margin calls. According to Mishkin (1991, 101) Kidder, Peabody and Goldman, Sachs had advanced $1.5 billion to their customers by noon of October 20. Fearing a breakdown of the clearing and settlement system and the large-scale failures of securities firms, the Federal Reserve System announced its readiness to provide liquidity to support the financial system, and it encouraged major banks to lend to solvent securities firms.

Monetary Policy Actions

Japan

During the 1990–1997 period, real estate values in Japan declined more than 70 percent, putting severe pressure on the banks and other real estate lenders. From 1992 to 1997, monetary policy in Japan was eased and interest rates were lowered to stimulate economic growth. Interest rates in 1997 were at the lowest level of any industrialized economy since the 1930s. The discount rate was 0.5 percent. The steep yield curve contributed to profitability of banks by allowing them to borrow short-term at low rates, and then lend those funds longer-term at higher rates. Some banks benefited, but others suffered and had to be bailed out and restructured. Nippon Credit Bank is one example of the latter (Lindgren et al., 1966, 66; Plender, April 1, 1997).

United States

In the United States, fears that foreign debt problems of less developed countries in the early 1980s might result in a series of bank failures and another Great Depression were a major reason for the expansion of monetary policy (Vaubel, 1994). From the third quarter of 1982 to the second quarter of 1983, the M2 money supply increased 14.2 percent per annum.

Nationalization

The term *nationalization*, as used here, refers to government ownership and/or operation of an organization. However, the share of ownership is not specified. The nationalization of banks is a technique used to resolve bank failures or to try to prevent them.

United States

Although we think of the United States as being a market-oriented banking system, there is a strong history of nationalization. The federal government owned 20 percent of the stock of the First Bank of the United States that was chartered in 1791, and 20 percent of the stock of the Second Bank of the United States that was chartered in 1816. By the end of September 1934, the Reconstruction Finance Corporation had invested $1.1 billion in preferred stock and capital notes of more than 6,500 banks, and they "owned" more than half of the nation's banks. For example, they reorganized Union Trust Company of Cleveland, with a $35 million loan and $10 million purchase of preferred stock to be matched by a $10 million subscription by common stockholders (Olson, 1988, 73, 81). In the case of Continental Illinois Bank,

in 1984, the FDIC and a group of banks injected $2 billion of new cap-
ital, and the government placed a board member on Continental's board
of directors. The FDIC owned 80 percent of the parent corporation,
Continental Illinois Corporation. Some might consider this a form of
nationalization, but the term *conservatorship* was used instead (Dale,
1992, 10; Goodhart, 1995, 408; Gordon and Lutton, 1994, 56; Wilmarth,
1992, 989).

Korea

The process of aid in the form of nationalization can be structured in
a variety of ways. In March 1997, the Korean Sammi steel group applied for court receivership. The state-run Pohang Iron and Steel group
had purchased Sammi's domestic steel bar and pipe business in an
attempt to rescue the firm (Burton, March 20, 1997).

Sweden

In 1991, Nordenbanken, which was 80 percent owned by the government and was the second-largest bank in Sweden, made large provisions for loan losses. Capital was injected, and the government bought
back 20 percent of the private sector stock in September 1992. Then
Nordbanken was split into a good bank and a bad bank. The bad bank,
Securum AB, was owned by the government, and it took over 60 billion
Krona of bad debts from Nordenbanken. The good assets remained at
Nordenbanken. The government injected $800 million into the state-
controlled Nordenbanken, to guarantee a $609 million loan to save the
largest savings bank. The cost of the recapitalization was 6.4 percent
of GDP (Caprio and Klingebiel, 1996, 36).

Open-Bank Assistance

United States

In the United States, the Garn-St. Germain Depository Institutions
Act of 1982 amended Section 13(c) of the Federal Deposit Insurance Act
to grant the FDIC authority to provide financial assistance to open,
ongoing insured banks "when in the opinion of the Board of Directors
the continued operation of such bank is essential to provide adequate
banking service to the community."

There are four types of open-bank assistance: the loan and investment programs of the Reconstruction Finance Corporation (RFC), the
FDIC net worth certificate program for savings banks, the FDIC capital
forbearance and loan-loss amortization program for agricultural and
energy banks, and direct open-bank assistance. Direct open-bank assistance was provided to First Pennsylvania Bank, N.A. (1980) with

assets of $8 billion, Continental Illinois National Bank (1984) with assets of $36 billion, BancOklahoma (1986) with assets of $1.5 billion, First City Bancorporation (1988) with assets of $11 billion, and others (United States Department of Treasury, *Modernizing the Financial System*, 1991, 1–34; *Failed Bank Cost Analysis*, 1991; *Resolution Trust Corporation*, 1990).

Payoff

United States

A payoff of insured depositors of a failed bank occurs when no acquirer has offered a sufficient premium to cover the costs, or there is fraud or other claims that make it difficult to estimate the losses in order to apply the cost test. In a direct payoff, the FDIC pays off depositors up to the $100,000 limit. The largest payoff transaction was Penn Square Bank, in Oklahoma City, Oklahoma, in 1982. Penn Square had deposits of $470 million of which $250 million were insured. About 25 percent of bank failures are resolved by payoffs. In some instances, insured deposits are sold to other banks for a premium (insured-deposit transfer), and uninsured depositors may receive partial compensation (modified payout) (*Failed Bank Cost Analysis*, 1991; United States Department of Treasury, *Modernizing the Financial System*, 1991, 1–32).

Cost Test

Section 13(c) of the Federal Deposit Insurance Act requires that the cost of assistance provided to failed or failing banks not exceed the cost of a payoff and liquidation of the institution. According to the General Accounting Office (1991b, 29), the application of the cost test has resulted in a higher probability that larger institutions will be handled so that their creditors and uninsured depositors are paid the maximum amount that they are permitted to receive under FIRREA (1989), which is the amount they would have received in a liquidation. This occurs because the FDIC is likely to become involved earlier with publicly traded institutions, which tend to have higher franchise values than small institutions.

Persuasion

United Kingdom

Johnson Matthey Bankers (JMB) Limited was one of five London gold bullion and commodity traders. JMB was a subsidiary of Johnson Matthey PLC. JMB was a relatively small bank, with assets of US$976 million. The bank's failure in 1984 was significant because it was the first one since 1975 (Jayanti et al., 1996). When the price of gold declined, the bank turned to commercial lending, which resulted in losses on the loans that wiped out most of their capital (Goodhart, 1995; Ollard and Routledge, 1985).

The Bank of England was aware of the problem at least a year before the bank failed, but did nothing to prevent its collapse. JMB's parent company, Johnson Matthey PLC, refused to provide enough capital to save the bank. However, it did inject $62 million, and Charter Consolidated PLC injected an additional $31 million. The Bank of England was concerned about London's reputation as a leading international gold bullion market, and stepped in to provide support for JMB. The Bank of England persuaded four banks (Barclays, Lloyds, Midland, and National Westminster), as well as members of the gold market and others, to provide £70 million to support JMB. Neither the Bank of England nor any of the other participants experienced any losses from the bailout. The problem had not been recognized or addressed by bank regulators. The result was the passage of the Banking Act of 1987, which dealt with bank regulation and supervision. The Act confirmed the Bank of England's role as a regulator (U.S. General Accounting Office, 1994b, 14, 45).

Persuasion does not always work. British & Commonwealth Merchant Bank (BCMB) was part of a large financial services group (British & Commonwealth Holdings) that had heavy losses in its leasing subsidiary, Atlantic Computers. Some creditor banks refused to renew a standby credit facility to BCMB. Then the firm failed after the Securities Investment Board (SIB) removed BCMB from its list of authorized banks, and it ordered SIB-regulated firms to withdraw their clients' funds. The Bank of England was unable to persuade other banks to provide sufficient credit facilities, and BCMB was closed in 1990. Depositors were paid 75 percent of their deposits up to 15,000 pounds (Goodhart, 1995, 406).

Privatization

France

In 1986, the French legislature enacted a law providing that the majority interests owned directly or indirectly in sixty-five companies would be transferred to the private sector no later than March 1, 1991. However, the date was extended. The French law was part of the liberalization of European markets. The European Commission (EC), acting as a rulemaker and referee in the process, banned continued government operating subsidies of nationalized firms. As long as state ownership exists, state subsidies take the form of overt grants, or low-cost financing. Profitable units within an industry may be used to cross subsidies to less profitable units. Artificially low prices for utilities are another form of aid.

The French government provided billions of dollars to support the operations of Air France and Compagnie des Machines Bull. These firms had huge losses, which made them unattractive for privatization ("Competition Policy," 1991; Cooke, 1993; Elliot, 1993; "France: Former Bull," 1991; McNevin, 1993).

Purchase and Assumption (P&A)

United States

A "traditional" or "clean-bank" P&A refers to the purchase of all or substantially all of a failed bank's assets (cash, securities, some loans, etc.) and the assumption of its liabilities. The difference between the value of the assets acquired and the assumed liabilities is covered by a cash payment from the FDIC to the acquirer—an insured bank. The acquiring bank does not have to buy assets that it deems undesirable, and it may return (put back) certain assets to the FDIC within a given period of time. In a "whole-bank" transaction, the FDIC sells virtually the entire institution and writes a check to the buyer for the difference between the value of the assumed liabilities and the value of the assets less the premium paid for the franchise value of the institution. The acquirer recapitalizes the newly acquired bank. There are two types of whole-bank P&As. First are those in which the acquirer has a contract with the FDIC to service problem assets. In this case the FDIC may have an ongoing exposure to losses. In the second type the FDIC has no ongoing loss exposure. Finally, there is the "small loan" P&A in which only some of the small loans are sold and the FDIC is responsible for the remainder of the institution (*Failed Bank Cost Analysis*, 1991; United States Department of Treasury, *Modernizing the Financial System*, 1991, 1–30, 44–45).

Restructuring

Japan

Nippon Credit Bank, the third-largest credit bank in Japan, experienced large losses. Nippon's affiliates, Crown Leasing, Nippon Total Finance, and Nippon Shinyo, had total debts of $16.4 billion. They filed for bankruptcy in April 1997. Provided that Nippon restructure, the Bank of Japan, commercial banks, and life insurance companies agreed to invest about $2.3 billion capital. The two largest banks involved in the bailout were the International Bank of Japan and the Long Term Credit Bank (Tett, April 24, 1997; Martin, April 14, 1997).[5] Part of the restructuring plan required Nippon to withdraw from overseas operations, sell key real estate holdings, close its Tokyo office, and reduce employment by 20 percent. Its president resigned. According to the *Economist* ("Japanese Banks: Rot," April 5, 1997), "By Japanese standards, these are dramatic moves."

France

Credit Lyonnais provides another example of restructuring. It was incorporated as a private bank in 1863, and it was nationalized in 1946. The French state held 80.7 percent of the shares in 1994. Credit Lyonnais is the country's largest bank. It had assets of nearly FFr 2 trillion and employed over 71,000 people worldwide. Under the chairmanship of Jean Yves Haberer (1988–1993), the bank expanded aggressively, almost doubling its assets, extending its retail network across Europe, and engaging in risky corporate loans and investments that turned sour. Credit Lyonnais had losses of FFr 1.8 billion in 1992, FFr 6.9 billion in 1993, and FFr 12 billion in 1994.

Credit Lyonnais has been downsizing to help resolve its financial difficulties. It sold some or all of its retail operations in Argentina, Brazil, Chile, the Netherlands, Peru, Philippines, and Sweden. Part of the bailout included selling 35 percent of its commercial assets outside France to generate cash. However, although the sale of Bfg in Germany will generate cash, it will also generate a capital loss because it will be sold below acquisition cost. Other asset sales include a book and record chain, a life insurance company, a specialist glass firm, a television station, and a hotel chain. The bank's chairman, Jean Peyrelevade, agreed to sell its Dublin-based financial services company, which provides auto and equipment leasing, that was acquired in 1990. However, he said that he would resign if the European Commission forces him to sell their operations in New York or Tokyo (Jack, March 24, 1997; Jack and Brown, March 14, 1997; "Commission Decision," 1995).

Reorganization

United States

Reorganization occurs under chapter 11 of the Bankruptcy Code. Under chapter 11, it is common practice for existing management to remain in place. The reorganization of First Republic Bancorp of Texas in 1988 is one example. Federal banking regulators allowed two troubled institutions, RepublicBank of Texas and InterFirst Corporation, to merge in 1987. First RepublicBank Corporation was the largest bank in Texas, with $32.9 billion in assets, when it was closed in July 1988. The idea was that cost savings might keep the two banks from failing. However, InterFirst's losses were greater than expected, and those combined with Republic's losses resulted in the combined bank's failure (Branch and Ray, 1997; Goodhart, 1995, 408; Gordon and Lutton, 1994, 56; United States Treasury, *Modernizing the Financial System*, 1991, 1–33; Wilmarth, 1992, 989).

Stock Market Intervention

United States

Following the October 1987 stock market crash, the New York Stock Exchange (NYSE) established a set of rules, called circuit breakers, that halt stock trading during periods of large price declines. This action was taken in response to suggestions from the "Report of the Presidential Task Force on Market Mechanisms" (1988). The Commission that wrote the report believed that such rules were necessary to permit orders to be processed efficiently. However, they did not impose the circuit breakers on increases in stock prices. This suggests that the purpose of the circuit breakers is to retard large declines in stock prices.

Commenting on the October 1987 stock market crash, Federal Reserve Governor Martha Seger (1988) noted that it was not enough to have the infrastructure of deposit insurance and direct liquidity provisions in place. The Federal Reserve also required the ability to shift policy quickly and flexibly to reassure market participants that regulatory actions would help prevent systemic financial dislocation.

Overview

Six methods of intervention appear to be common among the twenty-three methods examined here. These common methods include making long-term investments, providing short-term liquidity, nationalization, selling all or part of a bank, payoff, and waiting. For example, as shown in Table 5.1, assessability (#1), double liability (#2), source-of-strength doctrine (#3), and other methods (#9, 11, 13, 15, 16, 18, 22) require long-term investments. Similarly, bad banks (#4), bridge banks (#5), privatization (#19), and other methods require that all or part of the bank in question be sold. Some of the twenty-three methods, such as bridge banks (#5) and open-bank assistance (#16), involve more than one of the common methods.

CONCLUSION

The too-big-to-fail doctrine predates the failure of Continental Illinois Bank in 1984, and it is not limited to banks. Throughout the world,

Table 5.1
Intervention Techniques

Technique	Long-Term Investment	Short-Term Liquidity	Nation-alize	Sell All or Part	Payoff	Wait
1. Assessability	X					
2. Double liability	X					
3. Source-of-strength	X					
4. Bad banks				X		
5. Bridge banks			X	X		
6. Delay						X
7. Deposit insurance transfer					X	
8. Depositor preference					X	
9. Forbearance	X		Japan France	Japan France		Japan US
10. Holidays						X
11. State aid	X	X				
12. Liquidation				X		
13. Liquidity	X	X				
14. Monetary policy		X				X
15. Nationalization	X		X			
16. Open-bank assistance	X					X
17. Payoff					X	
18. Persuasion	X					
19. Privatization				X		
20. Purchase and assumption				X		
21. Restructuring				X		
22. Reorganization	Japan					X
23. Stock market intervention						X

governments intervene in the economy when they *believe* a particular event will result in severe economic distress, which they want to avoid. Stated otherwise, they will enact the TBTF doctrine when they believe that it is in their national interest to do so. What determines what is in each nation's "national interest" is beyond the scope of this book.

The TBTF doctrine has been applied to banks, industrial firms, railroads, real estate lenders, commodity brokers, and other types of organizations. Because banks are the main channel for the transmission of monetary policy and because of their role in the payments mechanism, they are the most frequent recipient of the TBTF policy. The criteria that governments use to determine which events qualify for TBTF are beyond the scope of this work. Nevertheless, the intervention techniques may shed some light on that issue.

Governments use a wide variety of techniques, individually and in combination, to aid the distressed firms and/or to reduce the cost of resolution. The twenty-three techniques used by six nations, described here, are used individually or in combination. Six methods of intervention appear to be common among the twenty-three methods of intervention examined in this study. These common methods include making long-term investments, providing short-term liquidity, nationalization, selling all or part of a bank, payoff, and waiting.

The chapter did not address the issue of the drawback of bailouts. Demirguc-Kunt and Detragiache (1997) listed the drawbacks associated with banking crises. (A TBTF situation may or may not be associated with a crisis.) The drawbacks include: the cost of resolution may be high; inefficient banks may remain in business; bailouts create the expectation of future bailouts; they may weaken managerial incentives; and loose monetary policy to prevent banking losses can be inflationary. Finally, in countries with exchange rate commitments, the loose monetary policy may trigger speculative currency attacks.

To the extent that TBTF is associated with banking crises, the chapter did not mention international efforts by the International Monetary Fund, or other agencies, to deal with global financial rescues.

No attempt was made here to deal with the welfare effects of TBTF. That is a topic for additional research.

NOTES

1. For a discussion of the changing definitions of insured deposits, see United States General Accounting Office, *Deposit Insurance: A Strategy for Reform*, 1991b, Appendix I, II, and III.

2. For a discussion of the legal history of the source-of-strength doctrine, see Pitt et al., 1994.

3. This Act amended Section 11(d)(11) of the FDIC Act [12 U.S.C., 18212(d)(11)].

4. For a further discussion of liquidation as part of the bankruptcy process, see White (1989).

5. According to Martin (April 14, 1997), the extent of the public and private bailout is $15 billion.

6

Prudential Regulation of Banks: Is It Effective?

THE CHANGING ENVIRONMENT

Bank regulators throughout the world face the challenge of regulating banks in a changing environment. The environmental changes include, but are not limited to, globalization of financial intermediation, deregulation (price, product, and geographic), financial technology (derivatives, securitization, unbundling of credit risk, etc.), and computer communications technology (Internet, electronic money and banking). In addition, there have been a large number of banking crises in recent years, especially in developing nations such as Thailand.

This chapter presents an overview of bank regulation, and questions whether prudential bank regulation is effective in its current form. *Prudential regulation* deals with the safety and soundness of financial institutions. In other words, it attempts to prevent bank failures. It also provides bank depositors protection against fraud and malpractice. Other topics covered in this chapter include the purposes of regulation, theories of regulation, problems with regulatory structure, regulatory failures, the cost of regulation, and the evolution of bank regulation.

HARMONIZATION OF PRUDENTIAL REGULATION

International banking regulators have undertaken major efforts to harmonize prudential regulatory standards. *Harmonization* refers to uniform regulations as well as to stemming the divergent standards that are applied to similar activities of different financial institutions. The Basle Committee on Banking Supervision, a committee of national financial supervisors, has led the effort to establish uniform standards. In 1988, the Basle Committee established uniform risk-based capital standards for banks, and other standards followed. In the European Union (EU), harmonization is reflected in a number of directives and recommendations. For example, the Second Banking Directive, adopted in 1989, established home country control and mutual recognition of national supervisory regimes. It also established a listing of banking activities subject to mutual recognition (see Table 6.1). In addition, the EU's Own Funds Directive and Solvency Ratio Directive are generally consistent with the recommendations of the Basle Committee.

Some countries are eliminating the distinctions between banks and nonbank financial institutions for purposes of regulation. For example, in France, the 1984 Bank Law eliminated the distinction between commercial banks, savings banks, and medium- and long-term credit banks. In 1990, the Banking Act in Switzerland was amended to put nonbank financial institutions and underwriters under the same regulations as banks. Similar legislation is also being considered in Canada and Japan (*Banks under Stress*, 1992, 51–54; U.S. Department of Treasury, 1994, 524–532). Nevertheless, national differences exist. In the United States, banks are defined as financial institutions that accept insured deposits, whereas in Europe they are defined as institutions that grant credit. Thus, General Motors Acceptance Corporation (GMAC) and General Electric Credit would be considered banks in Europe, but not in the United States.

THE PURPOSES OF REGULATION

Stigler's (1971) seminal article "The Theory of Economic Regulation," declared that the state has one basic resource that is not shared by even the mightiest of its citizens: the power to coerce. The power to coerce includes taxation, subsidies, control over entry, laws affecting substitutes and complements, and price fixing. Given the power to coerce, how does regulation affect banks? Kane (1988, 346–347) provides a starting point for answering that question by pointing out that regulation consists of efforts to monitor, discipline, or coordinate the be-

Table 6.1
Second Banking Directive List of Banking Activities Subject to Mutual Recognition

1. Acceptance of deposits and other repayable funds from the public
2. Lending
3. Financial leasing
4. Money transmission services
5. Issuing and administering means of payment (e.g., credit cards, travelers' checks)
6. Guarantees and commitments
7. Trade for own or customer accounts in
   a. money market instruments
   b. foreign exchange
   c. financial futures and options
   d. exchange rate instruments
   e. transferable securities
8. Participation in share issues and provision of services related to such issues
9. Advice on undertakings on capital structure, industry strategy, mergers, and the purchase of undertakings
10. Money brokering
11. Portfolio management and advice
12. Safekeeping and administration of securities
13. Credit reference service
14. Safe custody services

Source: U.S. Department of Treasury, *National Treatment Study 1994*, 531.

havior of financial institutions to achieve some greater good. According to the OECD (*Banks under Stress*, 1992, 31), the greater good includes:

1. Maintaining stability and confidence in the financial system by ensuring solvency and financial soundness of financial institutions (prevention of systemic risk);
2. Protecting investors, borrowers, and other users of the financial system against undue risks, losses, or other damages that may arise from failures, fraud, malpractices, manipulation, and other malconduct on the part of the providers of financial services (prevention of individual risk);
3. Ensuring a smooth, efficient, and reliable and effective func-

tioning of financial markets, including a proper working of competitive market forces (promoting systemic efficiency).

There are other purposes of regulation as well. Alan Greenspan, chairman of the Board of Governors of the Federal Reserve System (March 19, 1997), stated that the Federal Reserve is particularly sensitive to how regulatory and supervisory postures (e.g., capital, liquidity, and loan loss reserves) influence bank behavior because they directly influence the manner and speed with which monetary policy actions work. In contrast, Goodfriend and King (1988, 219) claim that there is a mainstream professional consensus that monetary policy can be accomplished without supporting financial regulations. The U.S. Treasury, in *Modernizing the Financial System* (1991, x), states that bank regulation and supervision helps provide a substitute for the market discipline removed by deposit insurance. More will be said about that shortly.

Thomas Hoenig (1997), president of the Federal Reserve Bank of Kansas City, asserts that maintaining the integrity of the payments system is a compelling reason for regulating banks. The payments system revolves around banks, and demand deposits are the principal means of retail payments. In addition, banks clear and settle almost all noncash transactions.

According to Schwartz (1988b, 39), banks should be regulated because their widespread failure could lead to a drastic reduction in the money supply with disastrous effects on economic activity. In emerging economies, banks bear the brunt of interest rate increases, and they are necessary to defend a currency. Therefore, Folkerts-Laundau and Ito (1995, 8) state that issues of solvency and liquidity in the banking system "quickly move to the top of the agenda in countries experiencing financial distress." As increasing numbers of emerging countries are integrated into global capital markets, they will become more vulnerable to external developments, such as cycle changes in industrial countries, and shocks in major markets. The 1987 stock market crash and the Mexican Peso Crisis of December 1994 demonstrate how disturbances in one market may spread to other markets (Folkerts-Laundau and Ito, 1995, 26).

Edwards (1988, 115–116) states that regulation should be used to interfere with the natural and competitive evolution of the market structure in order to prevent monopoly power. Moreover, if size, by itself, carries with it undesirable features, then it too should be regulated. In an historical context, American public opinion has always mistrusted large-size corporations, including banks. It said that Woodrow Wilson created the Federal Reserve to take power away from J. P. Morgan and his bank, which some believe had become the nation's de facto central bank (Roe, 1994, 40).

Benston (1986, 2) claims that most of the historical reasons for regulating banks are no longer relevant. The reasons he lists are taxation of banks as monopoly suppliers of money, the prevention of centralized power, bank failures and effects of failures on the economy, the provision of banking services as a social goal, support of housing to allocate credit as a social goal, and the prevention of invidious discrimination and unfair dealing against persons. Nevertheless, Benston and Kaufman (1966) conclude that the only economic justification for regulating banks is the reduction of the negative externalities from moral hazard and agency costs that accompany poorly structured, government-provided deposit insurance.

Eisenbeis (1986) reached a different conclusion. He stated that the rationale for restricting banking activities suggests that the traditional concerns for economic efficiency, safety and soundness, concentration of power, and conflicts of interest continue to be valid.

THEORIES OF REGULATION

Private Market Regulation

Alan Greenspan (April 12, 1997) said that the self-interest of industry participants generates private market regulation. The counterparties in a transaction scrutinize each other and require collateral and legal protection. Clearing houses and exchanges are examples of self-regulation. They establish margins and capital requirements to protect the interest of their members.

Continental Illinois bank invested heavily in wholesale loans. It had purchased about $1 billion in large participations in high-risk oil loans from Penn Square Bank in Oklahoma. Some of those loans were fraudulent. In addition, they had loans to less developed countries (LDC). Bad energy and LDC loans were fatal to the bank. Because Continental Illinois bank could not have branch banks due to Illinois state laws restricting branch banking, it depended heavily on uninsured deposits, a large portion of which was held by large institutions around the world. The dollar size of such deposits typically was tens or hundreds of millions of dollars. The institutional investors had a "silent run" on deposits in response to rumors of Continental's problems. The withdrawals reached $8 billion per day, far exceeding the bank's ability to meet them. Continental Illinois bank had assets of $41.4 billion when it failed. The market discipline worked, to a degree. However, bank regulators stepped in to rescue it in 1984 because it was considered too-big-to-fail. Its failure would have endangered the viability of hundreds of other banks whose funds were on deposit at Continental (Davis, 1995, 251; Fraser and Richards, 1985; Jackson, 1995; Wall and Peterson, 1990; Wilmarth, 1992, 988).

Market Failure Theory

According to this approach, regulations are created politically to provide a means to remedy suboptimal equilibrium that would exist in a private, unregulated industry (Garcia, 1992). Regulatory bodies are supposed to reduce the inefficiencies caused by market failures.

Market Restrictions/Price Competition

The rationale for market restrictions is that if price competition were allowed to prevail, it might undermine the solvency of financial institutions. Limits on interest rates that can be paid on deposits, such as Federal Reserve Regulation Q, are one example of price controls. By the 1990s, most major countries had eliminated such controls, and banks were allowed to pay competitive rates for deposits (*Banks under Stress*, 1992, 41).

Market Restrictions/Limitation of Powers

Market-restrictive laws lead to segmentation and the development of specialized financial institutions. For example, laws restricting banks from investment banking, such as the Glass-Steagall Act, led to specialized securities firms in the United States and elsewhere (*Banks under Stress*, 1992, 32; Benston, 1990). However, such laws that limited banking powers did not cause fragmentation of the banking system.

Fragmentation began in the nineteenth century. Following the destruction of the Second Bank of the United States by Andrew Jackson's veto of the bill to recharter it, each state established its own banking laws, which limited banking activities. According to Roe (1994, 58, 78–79), state banks disliked the Second Bank, which competed with them and could control them. Therefore, the states established laws, such as unit banking laws, that kept institutions small and protected them. When Congress created national banks, they were national in name, but local in operation. The politically strong banks also helped to keep some large New York insurers from becoming the first truly national American financial institutions at the turn of the century. Thus, American federalism contributed to the fragmentation of the financial system.

Regulatory Capture

Regulations are created politically to serve some distributional interest. Becker (1983) claims that government corrects market failures

with the view that they favor the politically powerful. Regulations, subsidies, and other political instruments are used to create, preserve, and
allocate wealth. In this case, the banks have a lot at stake, and they
play a significant role in shaping the legislation that affects them. For
example, Citicorp opposed proposed legislation in 1997 that would
eliminate thrift charters, because they had used a thrift charter to establish a $14 billion nationwide consumer banking operation (Mc-
Connell, October 6, 1997). Peltzman (1989) extends that thought and
argues that regulation is a way to allocate economic rents. Regulations
serve producers' interests, creating cartels that raise prices. Nevertheless, Peltzman points out that regulations that generated rents can be
undermined. In the case of financial institutions, they were undermined by product innovations. Thus, money market funds grew at the
expense of banks that had limits on the interest that they could pay on
deposits.

Deregulation

Peltzman (1989) claims that regulations create incentives for wealth
dissipation, which makes restoration of the preregulation status quo
more attractive than continuing regulation-deregulation. The relaxa-
tion by the Board of Governors of twenty-eight "firewalls" that sepa-
rated banks from underwriting activities is a case in point (Phillips,
March 20, 1997). This change and other forms of deregulation occurred
without changes in legislation. Mayer (March 28, 1997) states that the
Clinton administration and Senator Alfonse D'Amato's proposals to de-
regulate bank-industry combinations "would put an end to the greatest
extension of government intervention in the private sector since the
'Great Society.' " He goes on to say that technological forces of changes
will mold the industry regardless of what congress does.

The concept of making laws and then changing them is not limited
to the 1990s. Thomas Jefferson (1816) said, "I am not an advocate for
frequent changes in laws and constitutions, but laws and institutions
must go hand in hand with the progress of the human mind. As that
becomes more developed, more enlightened, . . . with the change of circumstances, institutions must advance to keep pace with the times."

PROBLEMS WITH REGULATORY STRUCTURE

The U.S. Treasury, in *Modernizing the Financial System* (1991, x),
states that there has not always been a satisfactory regulatory mechanism in the United States for the prompt resolution of banking problems. There may be as many as four bank regulators involved in the
affairs of a single bank, and no single regulator has either the full in-

formation or clear authority and responsibility for decisive, timely action that is required to deal with problem institutions.

Garten (1991, viii) points out that the form of regulations is often shaped by practical constraints on the agencies' ability to enforce particular policies. Although, in theory, some regulatory goals may be desirable, in practice, they cannot be implemented effectively. Therefore, proponents of changes in banking laws must consider how regulators can implement them.

A key issue in regulation is how regulatory agencies impose their controls on the management actions of privately owned firms that must respond to market forces. Their ability to impose controls is limited by significant costs for both information (monitoring) and enforcement. In the United States, monitoring is provided by on-site examinations, periodic reports provided by the banks, and securities market information for banks with publicly traded securities—typically large banks. Enforcement takes the form of regulations and the implied threat and use of disciplinary actions for the violators. Thus, Garten (1991, 24) states that the problem of regulation becomes circular: Regulation requires monitoring to detect violations of regulations. However, monitoring requires better enforcement of regulations in order to discourage violations. The banks have little incentive to aid regulators in their monitoring efforts beyond the minimum required by law.

Symbiosis

There is a symbiotic relationship between banks and regulators. Garten (1991, 147) finds that bank regulatory strategies that work best are those that contribute to the profitability of the industry. The bank regulators may be thought of as investors in the banking industry who seek to maximize their own investment. The most significant regulatory reforms in recent years have occurred at the agency level, where there has been a gradual elimination of banking products restrictions. However, government regulations involve some elements of perverse incentives. Greenspan (April 12, 1997) stated that "if private market participants believe that government is protecting their interests, their own efforts to do so will diminish."

Risk and Unintended Consequences

Greenspan (1993, 3) observed that the legislative and regulatory process has not adequately addressed how much risk is optimal. Recent banking regulations were reactions to perceived excesses, and they tipped the optimum balance. Greenspan cited the real estate appraisal requirements of FIRREA, which were designed to eliminate excesses in commercial real estate and development lending, but they also constrained bank lending to small businesses. Stated otherwise, toughened examination standards of the late 1980s were in response to lending excesses of the 1980s, but they also contributed to the credit crunch of the 1990s.

The previous example illustrates the unintended consequences of one law. Similarly, because laws tend to be long-lived, they can outlive their usefulness. The Glass-Steagall Act, which was enacted in 1933 to separate banking from investments because of alleged abuses, is currently a constraint on banking and investment activities.

What Regulators Need for Monitoring

Regulators need accurate and timely financial information from banks that they supervise, for the early detection of troubled banks. This requires sound accounting and reporting systems that fairly present the banks' true financial condition (U.S. General Accounting Office, 1991b, 7). However, the GAO (1991b, 43) found that even when such information was available, and despite the availability of enforcement tools, regulators were reluctant to use the tools because of their desire "to work cooperatively with management whenever possible," and "their perceived need to obtain irrefutable evidence of capital deterioration should their actions be contested." The Bank of New England is a case in point.

The lessons learned from the Ohio thrift crisis are that prompt, effective responses to public concerns are necessary to contain a crisis of confidence in the banking system. Prompt, effective response requires accurate information, understanding the extent of the problem, and the willingness and ability to commit resources to assure depositors protection from loss (*FRB Cleveland, Annual Report 1985*).

Commenting on the October 1987 stock market crash, Governor M. Seger (1988) of the Federal Reserve System noted that it was not enough to have the infrastructure of deposit insurance and direct liquidity provisions in place; the Federal Reserve System also required the ability to shift policy quickly and flexibly to reassure market participants that regulatory actions would help prevent systemic financial dislocation.

Limits of Regulation

Government regulations tend to lag behind market developments. In the United States, major changes in banking laws were enacted after the Great Depression and after the savings-and-loan debacle. Equally important, market participants find "loopholes" in laws to circumvent them. Accordingly, a Bank Administration Institute/McKinsey & Company study, *Building Better Banks* (1996), claims that new banks, such as Merrill Lynch, Fidelity Investments, and GE Capital, are not subject to the same competitive restrictions as old bank holding companies. Likewise, Bell Atlantic and Sears Roebuck gain access to the payments system through the banks they acquire. The changes in payments technology—the Internet and electronic cash—are outpacing regulations. Finally, competition gives rise to substitute products that may not be subject to banking regulations. The growth of money market mutual funds is one example. In summary, government regulations enacted in response to crises may not be suitable to meet changing market conditions.

Role of Government

Eisenbeis (1995, 73) states that there is a substantial body of evidence that government actions have played a significant role both in contributing to crises and in mitigating them. Friedman and Schwartz (1963) argued that monetary actions contributed to the duration and magnitude of the Great Depression. The Federal Reserve's failure to provide liquidity to nonmember banks and policy of lending only on sound collateral added to the number of bank failures that occurred. At the same time, following the rules of the Gold Standard contributed to a 33 percent decline in the money supply, which exacerbated the recession.

Monetary authorities rely on financial institutions to serve as an effective mechanism for the transmission of monetary policy. However, deregulation and the globalization of world financial markets has facilitated the circumvention of domestic credit restrictions. It has also blurred the distinction between banks and other financial institutions. (*Banks under Stress*, 1992, 36).

REGULATORY FAILURES

Meltzer (1995, 7) stated that one general lesson stands out from examining two decades of financial regulation, supervision, and deposit insurance and safety nets. In many countries, regulation and supervision did not prevent sizable losses by banks and the public. Although the amount of the losses differed from country to country, the effects on banks from real estate losses were qualitatively similar in the United States, Japan, the United Kingdom, Norway, Sweden, and Australia. The remainder of this section focuses on three relatively recent regulatory failures in the United States.

Failure of the Federal Savings and Loan Insurance Corporation (FSLIC), 1989

The fortunes of regulatory agencies are tied to the financial health of the regulated industry. So it was that the failure of hundreds of thrift institutions during the 1980s resulted in the 1989 bankruptcy of the Federal Savings and Loan Insurance Corporation that insured those thrifts. Congress reacted to the thrift crisis by abolishing the Federal Home Loan Bank Board, which regulated thrifts, and transferred its supervisory authority to the Office of Thrift Supervision (OTS), which now insures thrift deposits (Garten, 1991, 33).

Examiner Performance

The Government Accounting Office (GAO) reviewed seventy-two banks that had capital adequacy problems in 1988 (*Deposit Insurance: A Strategy for Reform*, 1991b, 5). They found that examiners often preferred to work informally with bank managers and directors to resolve problems because they lacked a clear mandate and incentives to take more forceful corrective action. While their goal was to close banks as soon as the equity was exhausted, the informal approach did not work. From 1985 to 1989, the losses to the FDIC averaged about 16 percent of assets. In 1992, the "tripwires," which require prompt corrective action with respect to capital adequacy, were enacted into law (FDICIA).

A summary of studies made by the FDIC (Hanc, 1996), concerning the effectiveness of CAMEL ratings 1 to 5, concluded that they identified most banks that required supervisory action well before 1,600 banks failed in the 1980–1994 period.[1] However, about 16 percent of the banks that failed were not identified at least two years prior to their failure. If only troubled banks are considered (those with CAMEL ratings of 4 or 5), the system identified only 46 percent of the banks that failed.

Some failures cannot be anticipated by safety and soundness examinations. Cross-guarantee failures, fraud, and failures of affiliates of certain Texas holding companies were outside the CAMEL system.

Bank of New England (BNE), 1991: A Case Study

Walter J. Connolly (1991), former chairman of the BNE, said that the BNE, created by the merger of two banks in 1985, "was the first superregional bank. . . . A New England Bank for New Englanders, positioned to survive in an increasingly hazardous environment." It failed.

Bank regulators publicly acknowledged that the BNE had problems in December 1989, but they were aware of problems as early as 1985. At that time the bank had assets of about $32 billion. Some of the assets were sold to improve the bank's liquidity and to cut its losses. On January 6, 1991, the BNE, with assets of $22 billion, was declared insolvent, and it was taken over by bank regulators. The insolvency included the holding company and two subsidiaries: Connecticut Bank and Trust, and Maine National Bank. Total assets were about $22 billion. This was the third largest bank failure in U.S. history, following Continental Illinois ($33.6 billion) and First RepublicBank Corporation of Texas ($32.7 billion). Weak economic conditions and faulty loans led to BNE's demise.

There were massive deposit withdrawals (runs) on banks in Boston and Providence following the collapse of the Rhode Island Insurance fund in early January 1991. The run on the BNE was estimated to be $1 billion in two days. The depositors redeposited their funds in other large and small banks in New England. For the FDIC, shoring up the economy and protecting depositors were of paramount importance ("For FDIC," *American Banker*, January 8, 1991).

On June 13, 1991, in a hearing before Congress (U.S. Cong, 1991, Serial No.102–49, 179), it was declared that the Office of the Comptroller of the Currency (OCC), BNE's primary federal bank regulator, "failed to accomplish their supervisory responsibilities." Their ability to meet their responsibilities depends on the evaluation of "sufficient relevant, accurate, and timely information." According to the report, the OCC failed to obtain the information necessary to determine the bank's soundness, appraise its management, or identify and follow up with corrective actions by management necessary to strengthen the bank.

In September 1991, the General Accounting Office (GAO) released a report entitled *Bank Supervision: OCC's Supervision of the Bank of New England Was Not Timely or Forceful* (GAO/GGD-91–128, 1991a). The OCC examiners were aware of problems with BNE in 1985, but despite the bank's loan growth, examinations were not expanded until 1989.

The GAO attributed the bank's failure to its liberal lending practices, poorly controlled growth, and concentration in commercial real estate in a severely declining economy.

THE COST OF BANK REGULATION

The cost of bank regulation can be measured in terms of failures, resolutions, and cost efficiency at banks. In addition, there are social costs that are not considered here.

Failures and Resolution

Individual Banks

According to a GAO study (1991b, 42), one indicator of ineffective bank supervision is the high level of losses that exist in failed institutions when they are closed. In theory, if they are closed when the net worth is zero, losses should be minimal. However, from 1985 to 1989, the estimated loss from resolving 896 failed banks was $109 billion, or 16 percent of their assets. James (1991) found that the losses realized in bank failures in the U.S., during the 1982–1988 period, averaged 30 percent of the failed banks' assets, and the direct expense associated with the closures was 10 percent of the assets.

Losses Relative to Gross Domestic Product

Goldstein and Turner (1996) report the results of an unpublished study by Caprio and Klingebiel (1996a,b) that shows the losses or resolution costs of severe banking crises in industrial countries: in Spain (1977–1985) losses were almost 17 percent of GDP, in Finland (1991–1993) 8 percent of GDP, in Sweden (1991) 6 percent of GDP, in Norway (1987–1989) 4 percent, and in the United States during the savings-and-loan crisis (1984–1991) 3 percent. In developing countries, losses were higher: in Venezuela (18%), in Bulgaria (14%), in Mexico (12–15%), in Hungary (10%). The most expensive crises were in Argentina (55%), Chile (40%), and the Ivory Coast (25%). Kaminsky and Reinhart (1996) report that the cost of the U.S. savings-and-loan crisis was about 4 percent of GDP.

Efficiency

A 1991 study by McKinsey & Co. estimated that a bank's total pre-FIDICIA regulatory cost for prudential risks ranges from 8 percent to 15 percent of its noninterest expense. Other studies by the Federal Financial Institutions Examination Council and by the American Bankers Association found that regulatory costs ranged from 6 percent to 8 percent of noninterest expense. The BAI/McKinsey report, *Building Better Banks* (1996, 7, 27, 28), estimated FIDICIA added two to three percentage points to the previous cost estimates.

Compliance

A 1992 survey of almost 1,000 banks that are members of the American Bankers Association estimated that the cost of regulatory compliance, exclusive of deposit insurance premiums, examination fees, and forgone interest on sterile deposits, was at an annual rate of $10.7 billion (*The Burden of Bank Regulation*, November 16, 1992). Part of these costs are due to the fact that banks are required to perform tasks that were once reserved for government. For example, the Bank Secrecy Act requires banks and other financial institutions to provide reports on large currency transactions in order to deter money laundering. The Community Reinvestment Act (CRA) compels banks to meet social goals that were formerly the purview of government (*Righting the Regulatory Balance*, 1992).

THE EVOLUTION OF BANK REGULATION

Traditional Regulation: The Role of Capital

External regulation and supervision of banks has traditionally taken the guise of establishing required standards, often in the form of ratios for such factors as capital, cash reserves, liquidity, and so on, and then trying to police these ratios. This section examines bank capital, which is the cornerstone of bank regulation. The term *capital*, as used in the financial context, includes both debt and equity. This may differ from *regulatory capital*, or that which is required by bank regulators. The ratio of banks' equity capital to asset declined from a high of over 50 percent in the 1840s to under 10 percent in the 1990s. During the early 1930s, when the United States experienced most of its bank failures, the average capital-to-asset ratio was about 15 percent, substantially higher than at any time since then.

Regulatory Capital

The Basle Committee on Banking Supervision, a committee of national financial supervisors, has led the effort to establish uniform standards. In 1988, the Basle Committee established uniform risk-based capital standards for banks, and other standards followed. The Own Funds Directive and Solvency Ratio Directive of the European Union (EU) is generally consistent with the recommendations of the Basle Committee. The EU's directive requires banks to hold at least 8 percent of their risk-adjusted assets in the form of capital.

This method of determining capital adequacy is recognized as a crude first step because it does not take into account differences in loan quality or diversification (Graham, April 4, 1997). For example, it does not distinguish between loans to a AAA rated company and one with a CCC rating. In addition, it does not distinguish between a portfolio of loans of 100 AAA-rated companies versus a portfolio of one loan to a CCC-rated company. Because of these and other deficiencies, other models that can be used to measure risk and determine capital adequacy are being developed by various banking organizations. J. P. Morgan's CreditMetrics is a step in that direction.

Purpose of Capital

In a competitive market system, private capital cushions debt and equity holders from unexpected losses. The debt holders are cushioned by the firm's equity. The equity holders are cushioned to the extent that substantial equity reduces the likelihood of bankruptcy. Thus, the capital markets "require" a certain amount of capital to maximize the value of a firm. The value of the firm will decline if it has too much or too little capital. The market requirement for bank capital may differ from the regulatory requirements for capital.

According to Berger et al. (1995), regulators require capital to protect themselves against the costs of financial distress, agency problems, and the reduction in market discipline caused by the safety net. The safety net includes the FDIC insurance as well as the Federal Reserve's discount window and unconditional guarantees of payments over the FedWire. It also includes the too-big-to-fail (TBTF) policy. Regulatory capital also insulates the economy from the negative externalities of systemic bank failures.

Miller (1995) pointed out that if the government is insuring banks with a TBTF policy, then it effectively stands as the creditor vis-à-vis the bank's owners. To be socially efficient, its capital requirements should resemble those in a competitive private market.

Benefits of Capital

Substantial capital lowers the likelihood of failure for the following reasons:

1. It reduces the incentive to take excessive risks.
2. It acts as a buffer for the deposit insurance fund and taxpayers.
3. It reduces the misallocation of credit attributable to the safety net subsidy.
4. It helps to avoid "credit crunches."
5. It increases long-term competitiveness (U.S. Department of Treasury, 1991, II-1).

Public Capital

The Reconstruction Finance Corporation (RFC) was established by President Herbert Hoover, and signed into law in January 1932, to revitalize the economy, but it did not succeed. Public capital, in the form of RFC preferred stock investments in Depression era banks, had three economic consequences. First, it raised the level of equity capital in banks thereby providing a cushion for depositors. Second, it was a substitute, albeit costly, for more volatile private capital. Third, it provided a signaling function because the RFC monitors the banks to control agency costs associated with management (DiLorenzo, 1984; Garten, 1994, 468).

The preferred stock was given equal voting rights with common stock, and it was not subject to assessment to restore impaired capital. The initial dividend on the preferred stock was 5 percent, but it was later reduced to 3 percent. If two dividends were missed, the RFC's voting power was doubled. This made RTC capital more expensive than deposits, because no interest was paid on demand deposits and the rate paid on other deposits was limited by ceilings that could be imposed under the Banking Act of 1933. It was also more costly in terms of corporate governance.

Deposit Insurance

Garten (1994, 468) argues that deposit insurance reduced the volatility of deposits as a source of funds. By shifting the risk from deposits to the FDIC insurance fund, the risk premium paid by banks to attract deposits was reduced. This encouraged the substitution of less costly deposits for higher cost equity. Hence, banks are highly leveraged. The equity capital-to-asset ratios of banks in the United States declined from about 25 percent in the early 1900s to under 10 percent today (U.S. Department of Treasury, 1991, 13).

According to Garten (1994, 468), public capital and deposit insurance had opposite effects on bank capital structure. Public capital tended to raise the level of equity, whereas deposit insurance tended to lower it. Another difference is that the high governance cost of public capital encouraged banks to reduce their risks. In contrast, deposit insurance created a moral hazard problem.

Market Discipline

Greenspan (April 12, 1997) examined historical evidence from U.S. history and concluded that in the future, as in the past, we need to place greater reliance on private market regulation. No chartered banks in the United States failed until massive fraud brought down the Farmers Exchange Bank in Rhode Island in 1809. Thereafter, a series of macroeconomic shocks, the War of 1812, the depression of 1819–1820, and the panic of 1837, resulted in large numbers of failures. In the absence of those shocks, the stability of the banking industry reflected private market discipline.

With respect to current times, Greenspan (April 12, 1997) concludes that rapidly changing technology is rendering much government regulation irrelevant. By way of illustration, he (May 3, 1997) points out that banks, investment banks, and insurance companies can no longer be viewed as separate lines of business. Although banks are prohibited from underwriting insurance, they can write put options, which are, de facto, a form of insurance. Moreover, other derivatives activities allow banks to behave as if they were permitted to merge with investment banks or insurance companies.

Recent federal legislation has placed greater emphasis on the role of market regulation. Provisions of the Federal Deposit Insurance Corporation Improvement Act of 1991 (FDICIA) impose higher capital standards, which shifts more of the risk to shareholders. In addition, changes in depositor preference for payoffs puts creditors and uninsured depositors behind insured depositors if a bank is liquidated. Nevertheless, most retail and wholesale bank customers do not have sufficient information about the day-to-day financial condition of individual banks to impose market discipline. In addition, not everyone agrees that market regulation works. A study by Nagarajan and Sealey (1997) found that reliance on market forces to help alleviate the moral hazard problem inherent in deposit insurance was ineffective in lowering bank risk.

Internal Risk Management

Today, bank regulators are placing increasing reliance on internal risk management tools such as Value-at-Risk (VAR) for trading portfolios, and similar measures for estimating credit risk. The reasons for this are that the increasing speed of adjustment of portfolio decisions and the complexity of financial contracts render ineffective those external controls that depend on the historical data-based measures used by bank regulators. Moreover, Goodhart et al. (1997, chapter 3) state that traditional accounting practices are too slow and inaccurate for tracing changes in a bank's net worth. Therefore, in the jargon of economists, regulators must devise incentive contracts that induce bank managers to behave in ways that have socially desirable outcomes.

The "precommitment" approach is one form of contracting being tested in the United States. This method requires banks to choose levels of capital; the regulators will fine them if their losses exceed those levels (Prescott, 1997). While in theory the precommitment approach is appealing, in practice regulators still have information problems because they do not know the quality of risk management capabilities of each bank, they cannot perfectly monitor a bank's adherence, and there is residual risk not accounted for by the models. It is clear that advances in financial and modeling technologies provide banks with new tools for risk management. Barings Bank failed because a rouge trader incurred large losses. Barings had a VAR model in operation. Similarly, derivatives losses at Daiwa and NatWest suggest that financial models are not the complete answer. Goodhart et al. (1997, chapter 2) state that the main issue for supervision remains the culture of internal management rather than its technical sophistication. Unfortunately, the measure of corporate culture is largely subjective.

Macroeconomic Factors

Even if there were a "perfect" regulatory process, it could be undermined by changes in macroeconomic factors. A former bank regulator said, "Yes, supervisors can help clean up oil spills, but they can't prevent them—only management can do that with the proper controls," (*Building Better Banks*, 1996, 71). The cause of most bank failures is loans that went bad. Within that broad category, real estate loans stand out because they have contributed to more bank failures than any other loan category. In this regard, macroeconomic policies have contributed to boom-and-bust cycles in Japan, the United States, and elsewhere that resulted in asset value deflation and ultimately in loan losses. Sheng (1996, 15) states that "the deterioration of bank portfolios and their rescue by central banks or the state have large monetary and fiscal implications because of feedback effects that lead to a vicious cycle of macroeconomic instability." Thus, macroeconomic shocks caused our most severe banking crises. Between 1929 and 1933, the number of banks in the United States decreased from about 25,000 to 14,000, a decline of 40 percent.

The Basle Committee on Banking Supervision's *Core Principles for Effective Banking Supervision* (1997) recognized the importance of macroeconomic policies. Their preconditions for effective banking supervision state: "Providing sound and sustainable macro-economic policies [is] not within the competence of banking supervisors. Supervisors, however, will need to react if they perceive that existing polices are undermining the safety and soundness of the banking system. In the absence of sound macro-economic policies, banking supervisors will be faced with a virtually impossible task." Even if governments attempt to have stable macroeconomic policies, external factors over which they have no control can raise havoc with banks. The impact of oil shocks and speculative attacks on currency, such as occurred in the European exchange market in the early 1990s, are two examples.[2]

CONCLUSION

The environment in which banks operate is changing, and the process of prudential regulation of banks must change with it. In the past, bank regulations tended to be national in scope, now they must be international. In the past, regulators relied on external examinations of bank capital, liquidity, and other ratios. If a major goal of bank regulation is to prevent systemic crises, the process was not satisfactory in the United States, but elsewhere it seemed to work in varying degrees. In previous chapters it was noted that France and Japan, for example, used various methods to assist some banks so that they did not "fail." In all fairness, the major banking problems in the United States were related to macroeconomic and tax factors that can undermine any bank regulatory system.

Today, because of the environmental changes that are taking place, bank regulators are experimenting with internal control systems. The strengths and weaknesses of the new system have yet to be tested by macroeconomic shocks.

NOTES

1. Bank regulators use a CAMEL scoring system to rate banks' condition. CAMEL stands for Capital, Asset quality, Management, Earnings, and Liquidity. The best score is 1; the worst is 5.

2. The impact of oil shocks on the economy was a major factor affecting banks in the U.S. Southwest in the 1980s. For a discussion of speculative currency attacks in Europe, 1992–1993, see Gerlach and Smets (1994).

7

Crisis in Thailand: A Case Study[1]

In the mid-1990s, Indonesia, Hong Kong, Korea, Malaysia, the Philippines, Singapore, and Thailand underwent economic crises for similar reasons, but each country handled its problem differently. Thailand had the first and most severe crisis, and it is the subject of this chapter. The crisis in Thailand provides a case study of what happens when there are speculative bubbles in the real estate sector of the economy, inadequate bank supervision, and ineptitude on the part of the central bank. The problem was exacerbated because Thailand's currency was tied to a strong U.S. dollar.

The chapter is divided into three parts. The first part provides a general description of Thailand. The next part examines the growth, prosperity, and real estate bubble that ultimately burst. The final part examines the lessons to be learned from these crises.

THAILAND

The Kingdom of Thailand, located in Southeast Asia, has a population of about sixty million people, and the country is about the size of Texas. It is a constitutional monarchy. Its major markets include the United States, Japan, Singapore, and Hong Kong. The Thai legal system combines traditional Thai civil law and Western laws. However, their legal system was not designed to deal with modern financial institutions. For example, their laws impede efforts to restructure companies and liquidate real estate. In addition, their bankruptcy laws do not adequately protect creditors.

Commercial banks are the largest financial institutions in Thailand. There are fifteen domestic banks, of which the three largest banks account for more than half of the market. There are also five special-purpose banks that finance particular sectors of the economy, such as agriculture and private housing. In December 1996, real estate loans accounted for 8.8 percent of their total loans.[2]

Ninety-one finance and securities companies are the second most important group of financial institutions. These companies specialize in real estate lending, financial lease and hire-purchase (car leasing) activities, and securities (margin lending) activities. Real estate loans accounted for about 24 percent of finance companies loans. They also accounted for 46 percent of total loans to the real estate sector at the end of 1996, compared to 35 percent three years earlier. Unlike banks, finance companies do not have checking or savings deposits, or provide trade finance. They fund their activities through short-term fixed-rate deposits and notes. Thus, they borrow short-term and lend long-term, a prescription for disaster.

Finally, real-estate finance companies (*credit-froncier*) finance the purchase of real estate. These firms are financed primarily with long-term debt.

There is no formal deposit insurance scheme in Thailand. However, the Financial Institutions Development Fund collects annual contributions from all financial institutions at a rate of 0.1 percent of deposits.

GROWTH, PROSPERITY, AND BUBBLES

Labor Costs

During the 1970–1990 period, Thailand had a competitive advantage in low labor costs. Low-cost labor produced clothing, shoes, and other labor-intensive goods for export. Except for economic problems in the mid-1980s associated with oil price shocks, the exports brought growth and prosperity. In the late 1980s, Thailand was one of the fastest-growing economies in the world!

Unfortunately, Thailand did not have a sustainable competitive advantage in low labor costs. Factories in China produced low-cost goods at prices that undermined Thailand's ability to compete in low-cost manufacturing. In 1994, China devalued the yuan against the dollar, which facilitated Chinese exports. In Japan, monetary authorities cut interest rates and weakened the yen in the early 1990s in order to boost Japanese exports.

Because of the changing dynamics of the market, Thailand was forced to move toward more sophisticated manufacturing. It attracted Seagate Technology, which produces disk drives. Likewise, Mitsubishi Motors Corporation, Bridgestone Corporation, and Komatsu produce automobiles, tires, and construction machinery, respectively, in Thailand. The latter three companies are Japanese, suggesting that Japan had invested heavily in Thailand. Despite their success in attracting sophisticated manufacturing, such as electronics and household appliances, international competition to attract such firms is intense.

A shortage of skilled labor resulted in increased labor costs. General Motors, for example, is investing $750 million in a factory in Thailand to produce automobiles, but it has to send 500 Thai employees overseas for training ("South-East Asia's Learning Difficulties," *The Economist*, August 16, 1997, 30).

Exports declined as a result of the rising costs and increasing competition. According to data from Krung Thai Bank, export growth was a negative 0.1 percent in 1996, compared to 23.6 percent in the previous year. The slowdown in economic growth in Thailand was not unique. World trade slowed in 1996. The International Monetary Fund (IMF) estimated the growth of world trade in 1996 was 6.4 percent compared to 8.7 percent in 1995.

Foreign Capital

The strong demand for foreign goods was reflected in Thailand's current account deficit, which increased from 5.1 percent of the gross domestic product (GDP) in 1993 to over 8 percent in 1995 and 1996.

In the early 1990s, the Bank of Thailand implemented a comprehensive program of financial reforms, including deregulation. According to the Bank of Thailand, the deregulation "program was carefully designed to ensure that local financial institutions are well prepared for the new competitive environment."[3] Perhaps more important is that this fast-growing economy with large current account deficits needed substantial inflows of foreign capital to sustain its domestic growth. The deregulation was one effort to attract foreign capital.

Part of the deregulation program included the establishment of offshore banking facilities, Bangkok International Banking Facilities (BIBFs). The purpose of BIBFs was to facilitate the flow of investment funds into the country. Deregulation also permitted the expansion of bank branches. By the end of 1994, there were 2,870 branches, subbranches, and agencies.

Many firms in Thailand borrowed heavily in foreign currencies, mostly U.S. dollars, to finance their growth. From 1991 to 1996, the ratio of external debt to GDP increased from 41 percent to 51 percent. Most of the firms did not hedge their foreign exchange risk because they believed that the government would defend the baht. They were wrong!

Real Estate

The early 1990s was a period of easy money and aggressive lending in the real estate sector by banks and finance companies. In 1993 and 1994, for example, the money supply (M1) grew at 18.6 percent and 17.0 percent, respectively. Total loans grew at 21.9 percent and 30.1 percent during the same period.[4] Banks and finance companies borrowed dollars, converted to bahts, added 7 percent on to their borrowing costs, and lent the funds for real estate and consumer loans. One report stated that "the forest of [building] cranes dominated the skyline" (Butler, *U.S. News*, July 28, 1997). More than 300,000 housing units were built that were unoccupied. In a good year, 120,000 new housing units are needed. The world's tallest building was empty. There was excess capacity in luxury hotels. The growth rate of construction peaked at 13.8 percent in 1994, and then slowed to 8 percent by 1997 when the real estate bubble burst.

Estimates of nonperforming loans (real estate and other loans) in 1997 ranged from 9 percent to 14 percent or more of total loans outstanding at commercial banks and 30 percent of the loans outstanding at finance companies. Because banks and finance companies understate nonperforming and nonaccrual loans, and they have inadequate loan loss reserves (LLR), it is not possible to get an accurate number.[5] Nevertheless, in the aggregate, nonperforming loans exceeded 20 percent of Thailand's GDP.

In June and August 1997, the Bank of Thailand had suspended fifty-eight of the nation's ninety-one finance and securities companies.[6] They had to restructure their operations and/or merge with stronger finance companies or banks, and they had to increase their capital.

The government also approved various measures to support the sagging real estate sector. These included: the establishment of a Resolution Trust fund; the establishment of the Property Loan Management Organization (a bad bank), to buy loans from financial institutions; the establishment of a Secondary Mortgage Corporation and a law dealing with securitization; and other measures. These are typical of the government bailout methods described in Chapter 5 that dealt with the too-big-to-fail doctrine.

Pegged Currency

The Thai baht was pegged to a basket of currencies that was dominated by the U.S. dollar. The U.S. dollar accounted for 80 percent of the basket, the Japanese yen 15 percent, and the German mark and others 5 percent.

Because the Thai baht was tied to the dollar, it was affected by the course of interest rates in the United States. During the 1992–1993 period, the Federal Reserve kept interest rates low to help U.S. banks and thrifts strengthen their balance sheets. The discount rates at the Federal Reserve Bank of New York were 3.25 percent and 3.00 percent in 1992 and 1993, respectively. Thus, for several years, the nominal exchange rate vis-à-vis the U.S. dollar was stable. However, in terms of the real exchange rate that takes inflation into account, the baht appreciated against the dollar. During that same period, the Japanese yen depreciated against the dollar. The result was that the baht appreciated more against the yen than against the dollar.

Dr. Yoshio Suzuki, member of the House of Representatives of Japan (1997), in discussing Thailand, Malaysia, and Indonesia, said:

> This appreciation in real terms against the currencies of the two major capital exporting countries, under systems that were nominally pegged against the dollar, attracted massive inflows of capital and caused domestic economic booms. The other consequences of this process were (A) the loss of aggregate demand control, (B) a further increase in the current account deficits, and (C) real estate bubbles. These three factors, together with (D) over-valued currencies and (E) deregulation of international financial transactions, provided sufficient motive for international speculation against the currencies. These five conditions were most extreme in the case of Thailand. That is why the Thai baht was attacked first, followed by substantial declines in the value of the Malaysian ringgit and the Indonesian rupiah.

The increased strength of the U.S. dollar against the yen and German mark in 1996–1997 adversely affected the value of bahts that were tied to it. Thai exports were no longer competitive because of the rising cost of labor. Stated otherwise, the baht was overvalued relative to Thailand's economy. The Thai government depleted its foreign currency reserves, spending more than $5 billion to combat currency speculators who were short-selling the falling baht. Part of the government's defense was to raise the interest rates that banks charge each other to 40 percent in order to entice them to buy bahts. In addition, they tried to cut off off-shore borrowers' supply of bahts. However, in July 1997, the Bank of Thailand (the central bank) unpegged the baht from the U.S. dollar and allowed the baht to float. At that time the exchange rate was about 25 bahts/U.S. dollar. The Bank of Thailand tried to support the baht until early July. Then it let the value collapse to 29 bahts/U.S. dollar. By early November 1997, the value reached an historic low of 42 bahts/U.S. dollar.

The Economy

The economy was subjected to a number of economic policy changes during the mid-1990s. In mid-1995, monetary authorities imposed a restrictive monetary policy to control inflation. The growth rate of the money supply (M1) slowed from 17.1 percent in 1995 to 12.1 percent the following year. The inflation rate was 5.7 percent in 1995, and the interest rate was 13.75 percent. The real growth in GDP slowed from 8.6 percent in 1995 to 6.4 percent in 1996. Then economic policy changed, and the money supply increased 20.5 percent in 1996. There was another reversal of policy in 1997, when the money supply slowed to an estimated 12.0 percent in 1997.

Fiscal policies also changed. The 1996 budget increased by 11 billion baht, contributing to inflation and the current account deficit. In addition, tariffs on selected luxury goods were reduced, hurting some domestic industries.

The stock market is a mirror of investor sentiment about the economy. During the 1990–1992 period, increases in stock prices reflected the rapid growth of the economy. However, in 1996, concerns about the economy were reflected in lower stock prices. In 1997, the stock market crashed. The plummeting stock market and the currency crisis that began in Thailand during the early summer spread to other financial markets throughout the world in October 1997.

International Monetary Fund

In August 1997, the IMF agreed to provide a $17 billion emergency international financial package, including loans and standby credits as well as technical assistance. The loans and standby credits would come from the IMF, the World Bank, the Asian Development Bank, and the Bank for International Settlements. The IMF's recovery plan involves balancing the budget, retaining the managed float of the baht, and closing insolvent financial institutions. Other features include strengthening bank regulation and supervision, eliminating government support of ailing institutions, and ending subsidies of state enterprises.

LESSONS

According to Yoshio Suzuki (1997), the fact that Thailand pegged its currency, instead of letting it float, contributed to the baht being over-valued. This, in turn, resulted in a loss of control of aggregate demand in the economy, it resulted in increased current account deficits, and it resulted in capital inflows that financed an asset price bubble. The partial deregulation of the financial system, without controls over aggregate demand or strengthening of the safety net of the payments system, may have triggered the instability that occurred.

Nobel laureate Gary Becker (1997) claims that fragile economies and floating exchange rates do not mix well. With floating exchange rates, the value rises and falls as a nation's competitive position changes. However, nations can debase their currency by printing more money. Inflation depreciates the value of currencies to maintain parity between the cost of domestic goods and their cost in other countries. On the other hand, fixed exchange rates require local markets to adjust to changing competitive conditions. By eliminating inflationary expansions and having a stable monetary environment, they work well for countries whose governments do not act responsibly in fiscal and monetary matters. Becker cites Hong Kong as one example.

What role did banks and finance companies play in this debacle? The speculators wanted to borrow money and the banks and finance companies wanted to make loans. In some cases, government intervened in the lending process by directing lending to create jobs, to increase industrialization, or because of political and personal relationships. When the Finance Ministry took control of Bangkok Bank of Commerce in 1995 because of bad loans, it was revealed that most of the loans were made to politicians. Thus, there were little or no controls over credit quality or loan concentration in the real estate sector.[7] In April 1997, Malaysia, which also experienced a real estate bubble, capped commercial bank loans to the real estate sector at 20 percent of total loans. However, banks are not the only financial institutions making real estate loans.

The Bank of Thailand, the central bank, is charged with supervising financial institutions to ensure that they are secure and supportive of economic development. It also formulates monetary policy and makes economic policy recommendations to the government. The facts speak for themselves, and the central bank was not effective in either task. By November, Thailand's Prime Minister offered to resign because of criticism of the government's ability to resolve the economic crises.

NOTES

1. Doowoo Nam provided valuable research assistance for this chapter and coauthored it. Mr. Nam is a Ph.D. candidate in finance at the University of Alabama.

2. Loan data are from Salomon Brothers, "Thai Finance Companies—To Be or Not To Be," August 8, 1997.

3. For additional information, see Bank of Thailand, "Financial development," http://www.bot.or.th/supervis3.html.

4. Data are from Krung Thai Bank PLC (http://www.ktb.co.th).

5. In March 1997, the Bank of Thailand introduced a 100 percent LLR on doubtful or irrecoverable loans, and 15 percent LLR for banks and 20 percent for finance companies on substandard loans.

6. According to the Bank of Thailand, on December 31, 1994, there were twenty-one finance companies and seventy finance and securities companies.

7. The Bank of Thailand imposed a maximum credit limit for an individual and related parties to 25 percent of the financial institution's first-tier capital.

REFERENCES

References for this chapter, which deals exclusively with the crisis in Thailand, are listed here instead of in the Bibliography of this book. Some of the sources listed here were found on the Internet. Where this is the case, Internet addresses are listed. Although it is the Thai custom to refer to Thai authors by their first names, here the family names are used for citation.

"Asian Prospects." *Washington Post*, August 19, 1997.

Bacani, Cesar, and Assif Shameen. "Devaluation 101: A Layman's Guide to the Turmoil." *Asiaweek*, July 25, 1997.

Becker, Gary S. "Fragile Economies and Floating Currencies Don't Mix." *Business Week*, September 8, 1997, 22.

Business Focus: Analysis of Thailand's Economic Recovery Plan. Board of Investment of Thailand, September 1, 1997.

Business Focus: Economic Restructuring. Board of Investment of Thailand, September 16, 1997.

Business Focus: Q and A on Thailand's Road to Recovery. Board of Investment of Thailand, September 23, 1997.

Butler, Steven. "It Was Too Easy to Make Money." *U.S. News & World Report*, July 28, 1997, 41.

Caves, Richard E., and Ronald W. Jones. *World Trade and Payments*, 4th ed. Boston: Little, Brown and Co. 1985.

Country Brief: Thailand. Washington, DC: World Bank, September 1997.

Financial Development. Financial Institutions Supervision and Development Department, Bank of Thailand, 1995.

Hall, Denise. *Business Prospects in Thailand*. Singapore: Prentice-Hall, 1996.

"IMF Approves Stand-by Credit for Thailand." Press Release No. 97/37, Washington, DC, IMF, August 20, 1997.

International Financial Statistics. Washington, DC: International Monetary Fund, various issues 1984–1997.

Kengchon, Charl. "Economic Overview." In *The 1996 Guide to Thailand* (Supplementary to *Euromoney*), September 1996.

Kochhar, K., L. Dicks-Mireaux, B. Horvath, M. Mecagni, E. Offerdal, and J. Zhou. "Thailand: The Road to Sustained Growth." Occasional Paper 146. Washington, DC: IMF, December 1996.

Krung Thai Bank [http://www.ktb.co.th].

Limthammahisorn, Watsaya. "Financial Crisis in Japan, South Korea and Thailand: A Comparison." *Bangkok Bank Monthly Review*, Bangkok Bank, August 1997.

Mishkin, Frederic S. *The Economics of Money, Banking, and Financial Markets*. New York: HarperCollins, 1992.

Muscat, Robert J. *The Fifth Tiger: A Study of Thai Development Policy*. New York: M. E. Sharpe, 1994.

"The 1991 Guide to Currencies: Thailand." *Euromoney*, September 1991.

"Recent Financial Developments." Financial Institutions Supervision and Development Department, Bank of Thailand, 1995.

"Recent Supervisory Issues." Financial Institutions Supervision and Development Department, Bank of Thailand, 1995.

Sachs, Jeffrey D. "Asia's Miracle Is Alive and Well." *Time*, September 29, 1997.

Seidel, Erica J. *"The Plaza Agreement of 1985,"* http://netspace.org/~erica/econ/, 1995.

"South-East Asia's Learning Difficulties." *The Economist*, August 16, 1997, 30.

"Supervisory System." Financial Institutions Supervision and Development Department, Bank of Thailand, 1995.

Suzuki, Yoshio. "What Lessons Can Be Learned from Recent Financial Crises." Remarks made at a Federal Reserve Bank of Kansas City Symposium on "Maintaining Financial Stability in a Global Economy," Jackson Hole, Wy, August 29, 1997.

Terdudomtham, Thamavit. "Year-End '96 Economic Review—The Economy." *Bangkok Post*, December 1996.

"Thai Finance Companies—To Be or Not To Be." New York: Salomon Brothers, August 8, 1997.

"Thailand—Crash of the Baht." *Pacific Rim Review*, July 6, 1997.

"Thailand Economy at a Glance." Board of Investment of Thailand, 1996.

Thapanachai, Somporn. "Year-End '96 Economic Review—Exports." *Bangkok Post*, December 1996.

"The 'Tigers' of Asia Stumble." *Los Angeles Times*, September 8, 1997.

Warr, Peter G. "The Thai Economy." In *The Thai Economy in Transition*, Peter G. Warr, ed. Cambridge, UK: Cambridge University Press, 1993.

"WEFA Country Profile." New York: Bloomberg, September 24, 1997.

"World Economy: Thai Crisis Highlights Lessons of Mexico." *Financial Times*, September 19, 1997.

Appendix: Bank Failures, Systemic Risk, and Bank Regulation

George G. Kaufman

Bank (depository institutions) failures are widely perceived to have greater adverse effects on the economy and thus are considered more important than the failure of other types of business firms. In part, bank failures are viewed to be more damaging than other failures because of a fear that they may spread in domino fashion throughout the banking system, felling solvent as well as insolvent banks.[1] Thus, the failure of an individual bank introduces the possibility of systemwide failures or systemic risk. This perception is widespread.[2] It appears

Cato Journal, Vol. 16, No. 1 (Spring/Summer 1996). Copyright © Cato Institute. All rights reserved.

George G. Kaufman is the John F. Smith Professor of Finance and Economics at Loyola University Chicago and a consultant at the Federal Reserve Bank of Chicago. This paper was initially prepared for presentation at a conference on Public Regulation of Depository Institutions, Koc University, Istanbul, Turkey, in November 1995. The author thanks Douglas Evanoff (Federal Reserve Bank of Chicago) and an anonymous referee for helpful comments on earlier drafts.

[1]Some argue that not only banks but all financial firms are potential sources of systemic risk. For example, in their study of capital requirements for securities firms, Dimson and Marsh (1995, p. 823) note:

> Implicitly, competition is assumed to generate appropriate capital structures, and the financial distress costs are an integral part of their decision process. Most countries take a different line for financial businesses, however. The systemic costs of default. . .have persuaded regulators to impose minimum capital requirements.

See also Davis (1992).

[2]The public fear of systemic risk in the financial sector and in banking in particular is intensified both by its relative lack of understanding of financial matters and by a constant barrage of fictional "scare" stories. Most persons are far more baffled and mystified about how firms dealing in intangibles, such as banks, operate than how firms dealing in tangibles, such as automobile companies, operate. Thus, they have greater difficulty distinguishing between factual and folklore explanations of the causes and effects of breakdowns in the financial system than elsewhere and their perceptions are more likely to reflect the greater fear generally shown of the unknown than the known. Superstitions gain credence. In addition, potential severe adverse contagious effects of bank failures and financial market crashes have long been a popular subject for novelists, who spin colorful and frightening stories, and movie makers. For example, the human blight caused by bank failures is vividly described in the best-selling novel of the mid-1990s, *A Dangerous Fortune*, by the best-

to exist in almost every country at almost every point in time regardless of the existing economic or political structure. As a result, bank failures have been and continue to be a major public policy concern in all countries and a major reason that banks are regulated more rigorously than other firms.[3]

Unfortunately, whether bank failures are or are not in fact more important than other failures, and I will argue in this paper that they are not, the prudential regulations imposed to prevent or mitigate the impact of such failures are frequently inefficient and counterproductive. Mark Flannery (1995) comes to a similar conclusion. The regulators have often increased both the probability of bank failure and the costs of such failures. In the process, the regulations have tended to socialize the costs of failure by shifting them from private depositors of the failed banks to general taxpayers.

In addition, the imposition of prudential regulations has identified banking as "unique," and at times has involved potential government financial assistance. This has often made it easier for governments to justify imposing other regulations that have primarily social and political objectives and are often in conflict with the objectives of the prudential regulations, e.g., credit allocation schemes.[4] However, the bulk of the evidence suggests that the greatest danger of systemic risk comes not from the damage that may be imposed on the economy from a series of bank failures, but from the damage that is imposed on the economy from the adverse effects of poor public policies adopted to prevent systemic risk. As a result, it can be argued that the poor performance of banking experienced in almost all countries

---

selling author Ken Follet (1994). More recently, the *Washington Post*, which prides itself on accuracy in reporting, published a fiction story disguised as a news article about the potential collapse of the world financial markets from a default by the U.S. Treasury during the budget crisis of January 1996, authored by long-time successful scare monger and best-selling author Paul Erdman (1996).

[3]Gerald Corrigan (1991: 3), former president of the Federal Reserve Bank of New York, has noted:

> More than anything else, it is the systemic risk phenomenon associated with banking and financial institutions that makes them different from gas stations and furniture stores. It is this factor—more than any other—that constitutes the fundamental rationale for the safety net arrangements that have evolved in this and other countries.

[4]Although not the subject of this paper, credit allocation schemes, which have been a major cause of bank insolvencies, particularly at state owned or controlled banks, in many developing and traditional economies, are not possible without a government safety net that removes the concern of depositors. Indeed, many authors, including Kane (1989) and Kaufman (1995a), have pointed to credit allocation in favor of residential housing in the form of encouraging long-term fixed rate mortgage loans funded by short-term deposits as a major cause of the savings and loan debacle in the United States in the 1980s.

in the last two decades reflects primarily regulatory or government failures, rather than market failures. Prevention of reoccurrences of the recent banking problems requires better developed and more incentive-compatible and market-assisted prudential regulation and reduced nonprudential regulations.

Implications of Bank Failures

A bank fails economically when the market value of its assets declines below the market value of its liabilities, so that the market value of its capital (net worth) becomes negative. At such times, the bank cannot expect to pay all of its depositors in full and on time. The bank, or indeed any firm, should be resolved as quickly as possible in order to treat all depositors (creditors) fairly and not allow a run by depositors holding demand and short-dated deposits. The longer an insolvent bank is permitted to operate, the more time such informed depositors have to withdraw their funds at par value and effectively strip the bank of its valuable assets. The entire loss will then be borne by less informed depositors and holders of longer-dated deposits.

In most countries, the failure of an individual bank should be no more important than the failure of any other firm of comparable size in the community. This is particularly true today when most bank products are no longer unique and are being provided in many countries by an ever growing number of nonbank firms that are gaining market share at the expense of banks. Moreover, to the extent that bank or branch office charters are not restricted, if the demand for banking services in the community is sufficiently strong, a new bank or office should be expected to enter. In the absence of deposit insurance, potential adverse effects to the community would be minimized, the faster the insolvent bank is resolved and the smaller the losses to depositors.

This is not to argue that bank failures are costless. Losses accrue to shareholders and most likely also to depositors, unsecured creditors, and the deposit insurer. Small loan customers may be particularly inconvenienced by changes in their loan officers, loan standards, and other aspects of their ongoing bank relationship. But this is no different from the losses and disruptions in firm-customer relationships that accompany the failure of almost any business entity of comparable size in the community.

What makes at least the perception of bank failures more important, particularly for public policy, is the fear that the failure may spill over to other banks and possibly even beyond the banking system to the financial system as a whole, the domestic macroeconomy, and other countries. Similar fears are generally not perceived for the failure of other firms. The failure of a steel mill, software manufacturer, or grocery store is not widely perceived to spill over to other firms in the same industry. Indeed, as Larry Lang and Rene Stulz (1992) note, the surviving firms frequently benefit from losing a competitor and being able to expand their market shares.

Whether or not bank failures are more serious than other failures, individual banks are viewed as more susceptible to failure or more "fragile" than other firms and the banking industry more susceptible to contagion than other industries. Banks are viewed as more fragile for three reasons (Kaufman 1996). They have (1) low capital-to-assets ratios (high leverage), which provides little room for losses; (2) low cash-to-assets ratios (fractional reserve banking), which may require the sale of earning assets to meet deposit obligations; and (3) high demand debt and short-term debt-to-total debt (deposits) ratios (high potential for a run), which may require hurried asset sales of opaque and nonliquid earning assets with potentially large fire-sale losses to pay off running depositors.

The adverse implications of this fragility are intensified by the fear that banks invest in assets that are opaque, illiquid and difficult to market, contain private information, and can change in market value abruptly; and the fear that depositors may run "irrationally" on banks, forcing unnecessarily large fire-sale losses. Thus, the greater fragility is believed to lead to greater failure.

Moreover, because banks are closely intertwined financially with each other through lending to and borrowing from each other, holding deposit balances with each other, and the payments clearing system, a failure of any one bank is believed to be more likely to spill over to other banks and to do so more quickly. Thus, the banking system is seen as more susceptible to systemic risk, where I define systemic risk as "the probability that cumulative losses will occur from an event that ignites a series of successive losses along a chain of institutions or markets comprising a system (Kaufman 1995b: 47).[5] A default by

[5]This definition is consistent with the one used by the Bank for International Settlements (BIS) (1994: 177):

> Systemic risk is the risk that the failure of a participant to meet its contractual obligations may in turn cause other participants to default, with the chain reaction leading to broader financial difficulties.

and by Robert Parry (1996: 2), president of the Federal Reserve Bank of San Francisco:

> Systemic risk is the risk that one bank's default may cause a chain reaction of. . .failures and even threaten the solvency of institutions.

Alternative definitions are developed in Bartholomew and Whalen (1995). The importance of defining systemic risk accurately has recently been emphasized by Alan Greenspan (1995: 7), chairman of the Board of Governors of the Federal Reserve System, when he noted:

one bank on an obligation to another bank may adversely affect that bank's ability to meet its obligations to other banks and so on down the chain of banks and beyond.

In a recent review of the literature on bank contagion, I identified five reasons that have been cited for more serious contagion in banking than in other industries (Kaufman 1994). In banking, contagion is perceived to (1) occur faster; (2) spread more widely within the industry; (3) result in a larger number of failures; (4) result in larger losses to creditors (depositors) at failed firms; and (5) spread more beyond the banking industry to other sectors, the macroeconomy, and other countries. I concluded that the evidence suggests that, while contagion in banking may be faster, be more likely to spread to a larger percent of the industry, lead to a larger number of failures, and be more likely to spill over beyond banking, losses to depositors at failed institutions—the primary transmitter of systemic risk—are smaller and bank runs—which can increase the risk by increasing the losses—tend to be informational and bank specific. At least marginal depositors are generally able to differentiate solvent from insolvent banks, particularly when they are given the incentive to do so by the fear of suffering losses. As a result, contrary to folklore, bank contagion on a nationwide scale has not been a common experience and, while large-scale banking failures exacerbate economic downturns, they do not appear to start them.

Nevertheless, the perception of both great likelihood and great damage persists and much extant prudential bank regulation is based on this perception. The remainder of this paper examines the potential for systemic risk in banking more carefully and recommends public policy initiatives that would greatly reduce, if not eliminate, this risk.

Systemic Risk and Public Policy

Although banking may be more fragile than other industries, this does not imply a higher breakage or failure rate. Rather, greater fragility implies "handle with greater care," much as it does with glass and porcelain objects. And apparently that is what the private market did in the United States when the proper incentives to encourage

---

It would be useful to central banks to be able to measure systemic risk accurately, but its very definition is still somewhat unsettled. It is generally agreed that systemic risk represents a propensity for some sort of significant financial system disruption. Nevertheless, after the fact, one observer might use the term "market failure" to describe what another would deem to have been a market outcome that was natural and healthy, even if harsh. . . . Until we have a common theoretical paradigm for the causes of systemic stress, any consensus of how to measure systemic risk will be difficult to achieve.

such behavior were in place. Before the introduction of government
safety nets, banks held considerably higher capital ratios and assumed
considerably less credit and interest rate risks in their portfolios. The
average annual failure rate for U.S. banks from the end of the Civil
War in 1865 to before the establishment of the Federal Reserve
System in 1914 was somewhat lower than for nonbank firms, although
the annual variance was greater (Kaufman 1996). In addition, losses
to depositors as a percent of deposits at failed banks were lower than
losses to creditors at failed nonbanks (Kaufman 1994). Jack Carr,
Frank Mathewson, and Neil Quigley (1995) describe the stability
of the Canadian banking system before the introduction of deposit
insurance in 1967. Anna Schwartz (1988) argues that until the recent
worldwide rash of bank failures—which are described in Herbert Baer
and Daniela Klingebiel (1995), Gerald Caprio and Daniela Klingebiel
(1995), Gillian Garcia (1995), Charles Goodhart (1995, particularly
chapter 16), and Zenta Nakajima and Hiroo Taguchi (1995)—while
banks failed, bank panics and contagion had almost disappeared in
developed countries, other than the United States, by the late 1920s.

Ironically, the introduction of government regulations and institutions in the United States intended to provide protection against the
fragility of banks appears to have unintentionally increased both the
fragility of the banks and their breakage rate. By providing a poorly
designed and mispriced safety net under banks for depositors, first
through the Federal Reserve's discount window lender of last resort
facilities in 1914, and then reinforced by the FDIC's deposit guarantees in 1934, market discipline on banks was reduced substantially.
As a result, the banks were permitted, if not encouraged, to increase
their risk exposures both in their asset and liability portfolios and by
reducing their capital ratios. As noted by Edward Kane (1985, 1989,
ana 1992), George Benston and Kaufman (1995), Kaufman (1995a),
George Selgin (1989), and others, this represents a classic and predict-
able moral hazard behavior response. Public (taxpayer) capital has
largely replaced private (shareholder) capital as the ultimate protector
of depositors. For example, in its 1994 *Annual Report*, the FDIC
(1995: 35) declared that "the FDIC remains today the symbol of
banking confidence."[6]

---

[6]Much of the general public considers the government to be the ultimate guarantor of
nearly all financial transactions, regardless of the size or type of transaction. In his analysis
of the Daiwa Bank's problems in the United States, Robert Samuelson (1995: 5), a well-
known economic columnist, writing in the *Washington Post*, noted:

> Financial markets (banking, the trading of securities) depend upon trust and
> confidence. Hundreds of billions of dollars of daily transactions occur on nothing
> more than a phone call or a computer key....In part, trust rests on faith that

Moreover, it could also be argued that the introduction of the safety net encouraged the federal government to impose greater risk on the banks. For example, national banks were not permitted to make mortgage loans before the Federal Reserve Act in 1913 and then only one-year loans until 1927. Likewise, the government did not encourage banks and thrifts to make long-term fixed-rate mortgages until after the introduction of deposit insurance. It is interesting to speculate whether the government would have introduced such risk-increasing policies in the absence of a safety net.

But, in addition, as repeatedly emphasized by Kane (1989, 1995a and b), the establishment of the Federal Reserve and FDIC in the U.S. introduced severe principal-agent problems. The Federal Reserve was charged with acting as the lender of last resort to the macroeconomy by, among other things, offsetting the impact of losses of reserves from the banking system for reasons such as a run to currency by depositors or gold outflows that threatened to reduce the money supply below appropriate levels. But the Federal Reserve was given discretion with respect to when and to what extent to do so. Unfortunately, as Milton Friedman and Anna Schwartz (1963) document, when the banking system experienced a run into currency during the Great Depression from 1929 to 1933, which dramatically reduced aggregate bank reserves, money supply, and bank credit, the Federal Reserve failed to inject sufficient offsetting reserves. As a result, the simultaneous attempt by nearly all banks to contract by selling assets led to large fire-sale losses and the largest number of bank failures in U.S. history.

To prevent another misuse of discretionary power, the FDIC was effectively established to automatically guaranty a given dollar amount of deposits per bank account. Most depositors would, therefore, have little, if any, reason to run on their banks regardless of the bank's

---

government regulators will supervise the complex payments system and police for fraud and financial failure.

Likewise, Robert Kuttner (1991: 28), another *Washington Post* columnist, ended his column on deposit insurance, the troubled Bank of New England (which failed shortly thereafter), and why he did not join the "irrational" run, by noting:

So my account is still at the Bank of New England. And my money is still at the FDIC.

Even some bankers do not believe that depositors should look only to their banks for safety. In criticizing the banking agencies' proposed capital requirements for market risk, Fox (1995: 3) reported that Jill Considine, president of the New York Clearing House Association, argued:

These standards are "unnecessarily rigid and extremely conservative."...The market risk rules should be used to "protect banks against normal market risks in their portfolios, [not] as a tool to protect the banking system against systemic risk."

financial condition. Rules were imposed to supplant discretion. But the law of unintended consequences was not absent. The absence of runs removed a major automatic mechanism by which troubled banks were previously closed and resolved. Runs on troubled banks caused liquidity problems, which forced regulators to suspend their operations until their solvency could be determined. In this way, depositors prevented insolvent institutions from remaining in operation for long and thereby limited the ability of these banks to enlarge their losses.

In contrast, after deposit insurance ended most runs, the bank agencies were able, for whatever reason, to permit insolvent banks to remain in operation and continue to generate losses. The failure of the late Federal Savings and Loan Insurance Corporation (FSLIC) to promptly resolve insolvent savings and loan associations in the 1980s, led to its own insolvency, the shifting of its approximate $150 billion negative net worth to the U.S. taxpayer, and a record number of thrift failures. Capital forbearance was also practiced in this period by the FDIC for commercial banks with high costs that were, however, able to be absorbed by the FDIC, primarily because a sharp fall in interest rates in the early 1990s, an equally sharp steepening in the yield curve, and new federal legislation requiring recapitalization of banks abruptly improved the economic health of the surviving banks before the FDIC's cash reserves ran out (Brinkmann, Horvitz, and Huang 1996; Kaufman 1995a).[7]

The forbearance not only contributed to increasing the cost of bank failures, but, by delaying the imposition of regulatory sanctions on troubled institutions, also contributed to increasing the number of failures. The average annual bank failure rate (1.09 percent) after the imposition of the initial bank safety net by the Federal Reserve in 1914 (1914–94) somewhat exceeds that (0.91 percent) for the pre–safety net period (1870–1913). This increased occurred despite a sharp decline in the nonbank failure rate from 1.01 percent to 0.65 percent. This suggests that the failure of the bank failure rate to decline likewise could not be attributed to increased instability in the economy or reduced market discipline, but rather to the adverse effects of the moral hazard and agency problems introduced by the poorly designed safety net.

Paradoxically, the Federal Reserve, the FDIC, and FSLIC used their discretionary authority in opposite directions with equally adverse effects for the economy. Friedman and Schwartz (1963) argue convincingly that the Federal Reserve was overly restrictive in the 1930s. In the 1980s, however, after the government had introduced a system that

[7]The FDIC's reserves were estimated to have been negative, however, if adjusted for expected bank failures and losses.

would prevent overrestrictiveness, not underrestrictiveness (which had not been a problem in the 1930s), both the FDIC and FSLIC used their discretionary powers to be less restrictive on troubled insured institutions than they should have been. In retrospect, both agencies were poor agents for their principals—the Congress, taxpayers, and healthy banks and thrifts that paid premiums to the insurance funds.

The Causes of Systemic Risk

To design public policies that can efficiently prevent the fragility of banks to be translated into a high failure rate, it is necessary to understand the potential causes of both individual bank failures and systemic risk. The causes of individual bank failure have been considered adequately by J.F.T. O'Conner (1938) and Fred Graham and James Horner (1988), among others, and need not be reconsidered here. The same is less true for systemic risk, although an exception is E.P. Davis (1992).

Systemic risk is perceived to occur because all economic agents are interconnected. This interconnection provides a chain along which shocks to any one agent are transmitted to others. The personal or institutional balance sheet of each agent includes assets that are either liabilities of other agents or whose values depend on the behavior of other agents. Likewise, the liabilities of each agent are the assets of others. If an agent suffers a decline in the value of its assets, the value of its capital will decline. This will likely reduce the spending behavior of the agent and thereby also the income and asset values of other agents. Moreover, if the loss in asset values were sufficiently large to exceed an agent's capital, it would cause the agent to default on its debt obligations. This, in turn, will reduce the values of assets on the balance sheet of the agent's creditors and ignite a chain reaction of reduced spending and defaults.

Losses to shareholders are generally viewed as less serious than losses to creditors, who are assumed more risk averse and often consider themselves not fully compensated for any losses they may experience. This is particularly true for depositors, who generally view these funds as the safest and most liquid component of their wealth portfolios. Thus their "harm" is greater and their response in rearranging their portfolios to avoid further losses is more severe. However, it should be noted that defaults lead primarily to redistributions in wealth rather than to aggregate reductions, as the creditor's loss is the debtor's gain. But the economic impacts are unlikely to be offsetting. The consequences of the losses outweigh those of the gains.[8]

---

[8]A more complete listing of alternative paths along which systemic risk may travel appears in Schwartz (1995).

Because of their continuous lending to and borrowing from each other and their need to pay other banks for third-party transfers, banks tend to be more tightly financially interconnected with each other than are most other types of firms. Thus, banks are widely perceived to be particularly susceptible to systemic risk, and shocks at any one bank are viewed as likely to be quickly transmitted to other banks, which in turn can transmit the shock down the remaining chain of banks. The adverse cumulative effects of the initial shock are intensified because bank deposits make up the larger part of most countries' money supply. As a result, depositors experiencing losses are likely to cut back on their spending by more than they would for an equal dollar reduction in other, less liquid forms of wealth. Such cutbacks will, in turn, reduce the income of other agents and thereby also their spending. Any impact of the reduced money supply, however, may be offset by deposit expansion by solvent banks that now have excess reserves or by the central bank through the injection of additional reserves.

Absent deposit insurance protection, bank depositors tend to be aware of the unique fragility of banks. If they perceive a shock to their bank or banks to be sufficiently great to threaten the solvency of those banks, they are likely to withdraw their deposits in anticipation of a default by the banks. Banks must sell assets quickly to pay these depositors, so that such a run is likely to lead to liquidity problems and fire-sale losses, which would both accelerate and intensify the transmission of the shock. Of course, for a given adverse shock, the greater capital a bank has, the less likely is it to default. In the absence of full deposit insurance, bank customers are thus motivated to encourage their banks to hold sufficient capital to avoid default from adverse shocks originating at other banks.

Runs occur in response to an actual or perceived default and, while they may hasten the transmission to other banks, Frederic Mishkin (1991) and Selgin (1992) show that they generally do not ignite the initial shock. The poor financial state of the bank is unlikely to have started with the run. Although popular in folklore, Benston and Kaufman (1995), Charles Calomiris and Gary Gorton (1991), and Carr, Mathewson, and Quigley (1995) document that history provides little evidence that liquidity problems caused by runs drove economically solvent banks into insolvency.[9] Benston et al. (1986) and Kaufman (1988) note that the effects of a run on the bank, other banks, and

---

[9]An example of the more common view is provided by Krugman (1994: 38–39), who states, without analysis, that in the 1930s there was "a wave of bank failures, which proved self-reinforcing as it led to runs on banks that otherwise might have survived."

the macroeconomy will depend on the running depositors' perception of the financial solvency of other banks. If they perceive some other banks in the system to be solvent and redeposit at those institutions, the effect of the run in terms of aggregate impact will be relatively small. There will be no or only little change in aggregate bank deposits or credit. Some adverse effects will be suffered by customers whose relationships with their banks might be changed or terminated, but, as discussed earlier, this is no different from the costly effects of any firm failure, and does not make bank failure a special public policy concern.

However, if the running depositors do not perceive any bank in their market area to be safe, they may flee into safe nonbank securities, most likely those of the federal government. Ownership of the deposits is transferred to the sellers of the securities and the implications depend on what they do with the deposits. If the sellers perceive other banks in their market area to be sufficiently financially secure, as is likely to be the case for the sellers to sell the safe securities, the funds will be redeposited in those banks. Again, there are no changes in either aggregate bank deposits or credit, only a redistribution of the banks holding the deposits. Adverse effects, however, may be somewhat greater than in the earlier direct redeposit scenario. Not only may some bank–customer relationships deteriorate, but the initial shift to government securities will bid up the prices and lower the interest rates on public securities relative to private securities. This may redirect investment from private to public sectors.

Moreover, if the perceived safe banks are located in a foreign country and the deposits are denominated in domestic currency, the first country's exchange rates will depreciate if the running depositors or receiving banks do not wish to hold the funds in that country's currency. The importance of this impact depends on the size and international openness of the country. For large countries, neither effect is likely to be sufficiently important to justify special public policy concern. For smaller, open countries, however, the percentage of deposits fleeing abroad is likely to be larger and the depreciation in their exchange rates is likely to be more important. If such a country attempts to offset the decline, it will run down its holdings of foreign reserves. To the extent the central bank cannot offset the impact of this loss on bank reserves, the country will experience a contraction in its money supply. Thus, for smaller countries, a run or a threat of a run to banks in other countries is more likely to be a special public policy concern.

If neither the running depositors nor the sellers of the government securities perceive any bank in any country to be sufficiently sound to warrant a redeposit, then there will be a flight to currency. The increase in currency held by the public will, unless offset by the central bank, reduce aggregate bank reserves and ignite a multiple contraction in bank assets and deposits. In the process, fire-sale losses will be greater and bank failures more frequent. Systemic problems are likely to occur. Indeed, it is a depositor run to currency that enlarges fire-sale losses and is likely to produce the major adverse effects generally perceived to result from widespread bank failures. In this scenario, banking becomes a special public policy concern.

Public Policy Remedies

What can public policy do to further mitigate the likelihood of systemic risk in banking and its severity if it does occur? For the sake of reality, we assume that some form of government deposit insurance, like central banks, is a political fact of life. Indeed, the evidence for countries that do not have explicit government insurance indicates that they generally have implicit 100 percent insurance. In the absence of permanently abolishing such insurance, there are three basic options.[10]

1. Policy can be directed at increasing macroeconomic stability and avoiding first abrupt increases and then declines (bubbles) in asset values and defaults. Schwartz (1988) and Goodhart (1995, particularly chapter 14) show that such instability has been a major cause of bank failures. Unfortunately, history has amply demonstrated that our current knowledge of macroeconomics is far short of what is required to achieve such results consistently.

2. Discretionary powers can be delegated to bank regulatory agencies to provide a safety net under banks to prevent both undue fire-sale losses from hurried asset sales by banks from affecting depositors and runs on the banking system into currency that exacerbate such losses. As noted earlier in this paper, it appears highly unlikely that such agencies, for example the Federal Reserve and FDIC, can do much better in the future than they have in the past in avoiding serious agency problems for themselves and moral hazard behavior by banks.

---

[10]All these options assume that the banks in the country start with a positive net worth or if not have, at minimum, a schedule for regaining positive net worth. These policy options do not deal with the issue of who pays for any negative net worth that banks may have—depositors, positively capitalized banks, taxpayers, or some other party. Kaufman (1997, forthcoming) notes that this is as much a political problem as an economic problem and the basis for much poor macroeconomic policy as many governments assume responsibility for the negative net worths and monetize this addition to their deficits.

3. Policy can be directed at avoiding the pitfalls of excessively discretionary and incentive incompatible safety nets and other prudential policies and focus directly on the cause of both losses to depositors in bank insolvencies and depositor runs on banks, namely economic insolvency of banks with negative net worth. Such a policy would attempt to reduce, if not eliminate, both moral hazard behavior by banks and agency problems by regulators by properly aligning the incentives of all parties in the same and appropriate direction. The incentive for banks to engage in moral hazard behavior can be reduced by requiring sufficient private capital and imposing a series of sanctions in the form of structured early intervention or prompt corrective action on troubled banks that mimic the sanctions imposed by the private market on troubled noninsured bank competitors in an attempt to have the banks reverse direction before insolvency. The ability of regulators to incur principal-agent problems is reduced by having them be required to impose these sanctions on troubled institutions and to resolve a bank which was not turned around by these sanctions through recapitalization by current shareholders, sale, merger, or liquidation before its capital could be totally depleted and losses imposed on depositors. The best way to reduce the costs of bank insolvencies to "innocent" third parties is to restrict them solely to shareholders, who may be expected to be more aware of the risks and be compensated for them more commensurately.

Benston and Kaufman (1988, 1994a), Benston et al. (1989), Richard Carnell (1992), and the Shadow Financial Regulatory Committee (1992) describe how many of the parts of such a structured early intervention and resolution (SEIR) program are included in the prudential prompt corrective action and least-cost resolution provisions of the FDIC Improvement Act (FDICIA) enacted in the United States at yearend 1991. Unfortunately, the prompt corrective action and least-cost resolution provisions of FDICIA as well as the implementing regulations were weakened by Congress and particularly by the regulators both before and after the act was enacted, so that failure and losses will be larger than necessary. In particular, Benston and Kaufman (1994b) argue that the numerical values for the capital tripwires are set too low.

The SEIR program focuses on the following six areas:

1. Explicit full government deposit insurance for "small" depositors. Full insurance would be provided up to a specified maximum amount per account and no insurance would be provided

above that amount. The precise amount at which to cap the insurance is difficult to establish theoretically, but should be near the level that depositors with larger amounts may be expected to have other investments that require the ability, knowledge, and experience to evaluate creditworthiness and may be widely expected to bear losses without much public sympathy and are unlikely to be able to conduct their business in currency and therefore run into currency rather than to other banks. These depositors would not only not be protected by deposit insurance, but would be expected to monitor and discipline their banks through market forces and thereby supplement regulatory discipline. Explicit full deposit insurance for small depositors is desirable, because (a) social externalities exist in providing a safe depository in the intermediation process for funds owned by agents for whom the costs of financial analysis of private banks outweigh the benefits, (b) these depositors are the most likely to run into currency and threaten systemic problems, and (c) insurance for such depositors is a political reality in almost all countries and explicit guarantees are more likely than implicit guarantees to avoid political battling when a failure does occur, which generally will result in the government providing full coverage and signal the willingness of the government to retreat in the face of pressure (Kaufman 1996).

2. Capital levels on banks that are equal to those that the private market expects noninsured bank competitors to maintain in the particular country. This provision is supported by Davis (1992), Flannery (1995), and Kaufman (1992). Thus, insured banks would increase their self-insurance to more market-determined levels.[11]

3. A system of graduated regulatory sanctions imposed on banks as their performance deteriorates through a series of zones (tranches or tripwires) that resemble the sanctions imposed by market forces on noninsured firms through bond covenants and creditor negotiation.[12] These sanctions are explicit, publicly announced, and become progressively harsher and more mandatory as the financial condition of the bank deteriorates through the tranches. (The sanctions introduced under FDICIA and the capital levels defining each tranche are shown in Table 1.)

[11]Merton (1995) identifies three ways for banks to reduce their risk exposures: (1) hedging, (2) insuring with others. and (3) a capital cushion.

[12]The effectiveness of private market sanctions in reducing moral hazard behavior on noninsured nonbank firms is examined by DeAngelo and DeAngelo (1990).

4. An explicit, publicly announced "closure rule" requiring the regulators to promptly resolve troubled institutions before their net worths decline below some low but positive critical level. The critical cutoff value of the capital-to-asset ratio should be sufficiently high so that, in the absence of large-scale fraud and unusually abrupt adverse changes in market values of a diversified portfolio of earning assets and liabilities, no losses are suffered by depositors or the deposit insurance agency. Losses from bank insolvencies are thus restricted to bank shareholders and deposit insurance becomes effectively redundant.

5. Risk-based deposit insurance premiums, both to discourage banks from assuming excessive risk and to prevent less risky banks from cross-subsidizing riskier banks. Because the closure rule should minimize losses to the insurance agency, overall premiums to be charged insured banks would be low and necessary only to cover these small losses and to finance operating costs, including monitoring market values.

6. Market or current value accounting, so that economic values rather than historical or book values are the basis for decisions by bank customers, bank managers, and regulators. This would also make for greater disclosure and transparency and increase the accountability of both banks and their regulators.

Although all six parts of the SEIR scheme contribute to its effectiveness, the key provision is the firm and explicit "closure rule." Indeed, no deposit insurance structure is effective in minimizing the costs from failures unless it includes such a rule. The prompt corrective actions increase the effectiveness of the closure rule by progressively increasing the cost to financially deteriorating banks of "gambling for resurrection" as they approach the closure capital ratio. The program must be compulsory for all banks in order that no banks remain implicitly insured.

The scheme operates more effectively if capital were measured relative to total assets—the leverage ratio—rather than to risk-based assets. This is not because the amount of capital that a bank is required to maintain by the market is not related to its riskiness, but because the necessary information appears to be too difficult to be incorporated accurately in the risk classifications adopted by the regulators. The risk classifications and weights adopted by the regulators to date have been arbitrary, incomplete, insufficiently reflective of the riskiness of the bank as a whole as opposed to individual activities, and modified to pursue political and social objectives. As a result, Elroy Dimson and Paul Marsh (1995) and Michael Williams (1995) demonstrate that

TABLE 1

SUMMARY OF PROMPT CORRECTIVE ACTION PROVISIONS OF THE FEDERAL DEPOSIT INSURANCE CORPORATION IMPROVEMENT ACT OF 1991

Zone	Mandatory Provisions	Discretionary Provisions	Capital Ratios (percent)		
			Risk Based		Leverage
			Total	Tier 1	Tier 1
1. Well capitalized			>10	>6	>5
2. Adequately capitalized	1. No brokered deposits, except with FDIC approval		>8	>4	>4
3. Undercapitalized	1. Suspend dividends and management fees 2. Require capital restoration plan 3. Restrict asset growth 4. Approval required for acquisitions, branching, and new activities 5. No brokered deposits	1. Order recapitalization 2. Restrict inter-affiliate transactions 3. Restrict deposit interest rates 4. Restrict certain other activities 5. Any other action that would better carry out prompt corrective action	<8	<4	<4

	Mandatory actions	Discretionary actions	<6	<3	<3	<2
4. Significantly undercapitalized	1. Same as for Zone 3 2. Order recapitalization[a] 3. Restrict inter-affiliate transactions[a] 4. Restrict deposit interest rates[a] 5. Pay of officers restricted	1. Any Zone 3 discretionary actions 2. Conservatorship or receivership if fails to submit or implement plan or recapitalize pursuant to order 3. Any other Zone 5 provision, if such action is necessary to carry out prompt corrective action	✓	✓	✓	
5. Critically undercapitalized	1. Same as for Zone 4 2. Receiver/conservator within 90 days[a] 3. Receiver if still in Zone 5 four quarters after becoming critically undercapitalized 4. Suspend payments on subordinated debt[a] 5. Restrict certain other activities					✓

[a]Not required if primary supervisor determines action would not serve purpose of prompt corrective action or if certain other conditions are met.

SOURCE: Board of Governors of the Federal Reserve System.

they provide distorted incentives, which differ significantly from those the market imposes, and encourage arbitrage within risk classifications. Capital should also be defined to include all bank liabilities that are subordinated to bank depositors and the deposit insurance agency and are not in a position to run. Thus, bank capital should give full weight to nonperpetual preferred stock and subordinated debt with maturities of, say, one year or longer, as well as to equity.

The benefits of a system of SEIR are substantial. In contrast to most government-provided deposit insurance schemes, this structure is both incentive compatible, so that all involved parties row in the same and appropriate direction, and market oriented, so that regulatory discipline is reinforced by that of de facto as well as de jure uninsured depositors. No institution would be "too big to fail" in terms of protecting uninsured depositors, shareholders, or senior management. By providing a number of triggers for regulatory intervention rather than only one, the progressivity of severity of the sanctions will be more moderate and both the likelihood and credibility of intervention by the regulators increased. Moreover, because losses to the insurance agency are no longer a major concern, banks could be permitted to engage in a wide range of activities, at least with respect to prudential concerns. The permissibility of the activities would be judged on the ability of the regulators to monitor their values accurately and timely for purposes of prompt corrective action and resolution. It follows that more difficult to monitor activities could be permitted banks with higher capital ratios. This flexibility would provide incentives for banks to improve their capital positions and introduce carrots as well as sticks in the structure. Banks would be risking their own private capital rather than that of the insurance agency.

If structured correctly, for any given degree of macroeconomic instability, SEIR should reduce the probability of individual bank failure, the cost of failure to depositors, other bank customers, and the community, and, by reducing if not eliminating depositor losses and the need for depositors to run on their banks, also the likelihood of systemic risk. The greater the macroeconomic instability in a country, the higher would have to be the relevant capital ratios for prompt corrective action and resolution to achieve these objectives. By itself, SEIR is not a substitute for stabilizing macroeconomic policy. Although reducing the likelihood of failure, the scheme does not eliminate failure, only the cost of failure to depositors and other creditors. Thus, the exit of poorly performing banks, which is required in any efficient industry, is not affected. Banks would no longer be unique and different from other firms because of any perceived or actual greater adverse impact of their failure and therefore no longer warrant specific public policy concern for prudential reasons. Benston and Kaufman (1996) conclude that restrictions on bank product and geographic powers that may have been imposed for prudential reasons may be removed and banks subject only to those public policies applied to other industries.

Systemic Risk and the Payments System

As noted earlier, banks are closely interconnected not only by depositing funds with each other and lending to and borrowing from each other (interbank balances), but also by making and receiving funds transfers from each other in the process of clearing payments due to or from other banks (interbank transfers). Because such transfers are frequently in very large amounts, are processed almost immediately, and are highly concentrated among a few large participating banks, the impact of defaults is more likely to spread quickly to other banks participating in the clearing process and is considered particularly disruptive as it may cause at least temporary gridlock in the payments system.

Defaults in the payments clearing process can occur when the payment and receipt of funds are not simultaneous, so that funds are disbursed before they are received. As a result, credit is extended by one party to another. In generic modern interbank clearing systems, payment for individual large value transactions may be made to other banks at the time delivery is made, generally electronically by wire transfer, but final settling of net outstanding balances at each participating bank is not made until day-end. Thus, for example, a bank may accept delivery of previously purchased securities, either for themselves or their customers, in midday and pay for them at that time even though it may not have the necessary funds on deposit at the clearing facility at the time. An intraday or daylight overdraft occurs. The bank anticipates having sufficient funds in its account at day-end through scheduled inflows to settle the overdraft, but these inflows are not certain and may not occur. If they do not and represent defaults on obligations from third parties and the resulting losses exceed the bank's capital, the bank in turn will default on its obligations to other banks. Because the same funds may be transferred a number of times among banks before day-end settlement, in case of default, these transfers must be reversed in order to identify who owes whom what. This process is costly, time consuming, and disruptive. Moreover, as described in Bank for International Settlements (1994), Robert Eisenbeis (1995), Flannery (1988), Baer et al. (1991), David Humphrey (1987), George Juncker et al. (1991), Robert Parry (1996), Heidi

Richards (1995), and Bruce Summers (1994), because the unwinding may result in losses that could cause other banks along the chain to default, so that losses cascade through the banking system, the payments system is commonly viewed as a source of systemic risk. A contrary view is described in Angelini, Mariesca, and Russo (1996).

To reduce the severity of such disruptions from default, some clearing systems guarantee or provide finality for each individual funds transfer as it occurs. The costs of later, day-end settlement defaults are then borne by the sponsors of the clearing facility (house). Such finality is more credible when the facility is operated by a government agency, e.g., the central bank, than by private entities, e.g., private banks. In the United States, an example of the first type of facility is Fedwire, operated by the Federal Reserve, and of the second type is CHIPS, operated by large New York City banks. Clearings on Fedwire are thus free of systemic risk.

Except for larger and more concentrated exposures, the credit risk assumed by banks in the clearing process is little different from that assumed by them in any transaction. Thus, basically the same techniques for reducing this exposure apply. The bank needs to know and monitor its counterparties, require margin when necessary, impose maximum loan limits, and charge a commensurately high interest rate on any credit extension. The bank's own risk of default is reduced by maintaining sufficient capital in light of its overdraft exposures. The bank may also delegate some of these decisions to the clearing house.

Until recently, the Federal Reserve did little to encourage banks to be greatly concerned about daylight overdrafts in their use of Fedwire. Because all payments were guaranteed by the Fed when made, the risk of default was borne only by the Fed. The Fed neither charged for daylight overdrafts nor applied bank limits on their use. As a result, Richards (1995) shows that the volume rose rapidly increasing the risk exposure to the Fed and, indirectly, the taxpayers. Since the early 1990s, the Fed has both charged for and limited the use of these overdrafts, but it has been reluctant to impose market-based charges for fear of losing business to competing payments systems. Moreover, David Mengle (1995) believes that the Fed may have provided a perception that it had spread the safety net under the payments system broadly by implying that it would assist banks experiencing liquidity problems on private clearing systems. In fact, as described in Eisenbeis (1995), the Fed provided such assistance in 1985 to the Bank of New York when it suffered a computer breakdown in its securities clearing operations and experienced a large deficit in its reserve balance. Thus, similar to the government guarantees on bank deposits, as structured, the Federal Reserve guarantees on payments system transfers in the United States appear to encourage risk taking by banks.

Ironically, the Federal Reserve views itself as a retarder rather than as an engine of risk taking in the payments system. Parry (1995: 2–3), president of the Federal Reserve Bank of San Francisco, recently argued that

> central banks do have responsibilities for reducing settlement risk. . . .settlement risk is a source of systemic risk. . . .Central banks need to worry about systemic risk because the private sector simply doesn't have the incentives to address this risk adequately. In fact, that's the very genesis of central banks' traditional oversight role in payments system issues. . . .There's a second role for central banks in reducing settlement risk. It stems from the unique advantage central banks have in being able to provide irrevocable, final settlement through the use of central bank money.

Similar to losses from bank failures for other reasons, the probability of a default by a bank and the magnitude of any resulting loss to other banks and parties from the payment system is reduced greatly if not eliminated by an appropriately designed SEIR structure. But, because of the large amounts, quick transfers, and high concentrations, additional precautions may be warranted to protect both the payments system itself and banks from defaults in the clearing process. The Bank for International Settlements (1994) notes that this may be done for large value transfers by permitting only simultaneous payments and receipts, or payments only in "good funds" against either other such payments, e.g., in foreign exchange trading, or delivery, e.g., in securities trading. This would eliminate the need for net settlement at day-end. Because almost all clearing facilities now have the ability to monitor in real time, such gross clearings for large value transfers are likely to be neither excessively costly nor disruptive relative either to the cost and disruption from defaults or to the long-run cost of providing an inappropriately designed safety net. Alternatively, Benston (1994) argues that market determined intraday interest rates may be charged for daylight overdrafts, maximum loan limits established for each bank, collateral required against debit positions, and participants in the clearing process subject to minimum capital requirements determined by the clearing house. To the extent the operator of the clearing facility is the government, the principal-agent problems discussed earlier are likely to exist so that appropriate measures to deter private defaults may not be imposed and resulting losses socialized. This suggests that economic welfare is enhanced if the clearing facility is private and its sponsoring banks subject to the provisions of SEIR.

A similar but more difficult problem to solve arises if payments are settled in different clearing facilities when settlement day-end is not at the same time at each facility. This is particularly likely for clearing facilities in different countries in different time zones. This problem was responsible for losses to some U.S. banks in 1974 when the Herstatt Bank in Germany failed and was closed by the German authorities after payment was made to it by U.S. banks at day-end in marks on the German clearing house but before it could make payments to U.S. banks at day-end in dollars in New York, which was later the same day. Because this problem cuts across different national sovereignties and thus laws, its solution is more difficult and requires coordination among the clearing facilities and respective governments. But as international markets evolve toward 24-hour operations, clearing in only good funds becomes increasingly feasible. Indeed, Philip Gawith (1996) and George Graham (1996a, 1996b) report that real time gross settlement is the solution recently proposed by a number of the world's largest banks and already activated on the London Clearing House Automated Payments System, or CHAPS.

Conclusion

The evidence suggests that banks fail. But so do other firms. Bank failures are costly to their owners, customers, and some third parties. But so are the failures of other firms. To the extent that failures reflect market forces, public policies to prevent exit harm other economic agents, such as competitors and those who will benefit from entry, including consumers of banking services. Nevertheless, bank failures are widely perceived to be more damaging to the economy because of the belief that they are more likely to spill over to other banks and beyond. Thus, almost all countries have imposed special prudential regulations on banks to prevent or mitigate such adverse effects.

This paper argues that these policies (both regulations and institutions) have frequently been incentive incompatible and counterproductive and have unintentionally introduced both moral hazard behavior by the banks and principal-agent problems by the regulators that have intensified the risk and costs of banking breakdowns. In the absence of such anti-systemic risk regulations, the greater fragility of banks did not often translate into greater failures nor did the payments system necessarily introduce greater risk for the banks. Indeed, the two periods of by far the largest number and greatest cost of bank failures in U.S. history occurred after the introduction of policies intended specifically to reduce cascading failures. The first occurred in 1929 and ended in 1933, two decades after the introduction of the

Federal Reserve System. The second occurred in the 1980s, 50 years after the introduction of the FDIC to supplement the Fed. Moreover, the average annual rate of bank failures was somewhat greater after the introduction of the safety net in 1914 than before and the failure of large banks occurred only in the 1980s. In contrast, the average failure rate for nonbank firms decreased significantly. This suggests that bank instability is more a regulatory phenomenon than a market phenomenon. As Schwartz (1995) has noted, omitting the government as a cause of instability in banking in a play about systemic risk is like omitting the Prince of Denmark from the first act of *Hamlet*.

Although systemic risk may exist without government regulation, on net, the probability of instability occurring in banking and the intensity of any resulting damage are likely to be greatly increased by some government policies adopted in the name of preventing systemic risk. This conclusion is not unique to banking. For example, modifying an analogy developed by Robert Merton (1995), just as governments may reduce the monetary damage from floods by providing information about water levels to threatened home owners, they may simultaneously increase the damage by providing flood insurance and encouraging the home owners to build and rebuild in flood plains. The latter adverse effect is likely to dominate the former beneficial effect. A similar conclusion was reached by the late Fischer Black (1995: 8), who noted:

> When you hear the government talking about systemic risk, hold on to your wallet! It means they want you to pay more taxes to pay for more regulations, which are likely to create systemic risk by interfering with private contracting. . . .In sum, when you think about systemic risks, you'll be close to the truth if you think of the government as causing them rather than protecting us from them.

Governments appear to face a tradeoff between two types of banking problems—potential systemic risk from the failure of one or more banks and non-systemic bank failures from excessive risk-taking and inadequate regulatory discipline. The first problem may be solved by introducing a safety net in the form of government deposit insurance and having the central bank act as lender of last resort. But if poorly designed or implemented, this solution is likely to increase the fragility of banks and exacerbate the second problem. Thus, governments appear to have a no-win choice. But the evidence, at least for the United States, is quite clear. The cost of systemic risk before the introduction of the safety net under banking in 1914 was far smaller than the cost of bank failures since then.

The counterproductive prudential policies have been imposed more in response to perceptions of systemic risk and "horror stories" in the popular press than in response to empirical evidence by public policymakers, who were responding to public outcries and were highly risk-averse. Similar to nuclear plant accidents, even if the probability of systemic risk in banking was very low, if it ever did occur, the expected losses would be very great, and reflect poorly on government officials and regulators. Moreover, through time, the regulators have developed a vested interest in maintaining and even expanding prudential regulations designed to combat systemic risk as they have become aware of the public prestige and power these regulations bestowed on them as protectors of society from financial collapse. In recent years, regulators have been among the most vociferous expositors and prophets of the dangers of systemic risk.[13]

[13]For example, John LaWare (1991: 34), a former governor of the Federal Reserve System, testified before Congress when he was governor that

> it is systemic risk that failed to be controlled and stopped at the inception that is a nightmare condition, unfair to everybody. The only analogy that I can think of for the failure of a major international institution of great size is a meltdown of a nuclear generating plant like Chernobyl.
>
> The ramifications of that kind of failure are so broad and happen with such lightning speed that you cannot after the fact control them. It runs the risk of bringing down other banks, corporations, disrupting markets, bringing down investment banks along with it . . . . We are talking about the failure that could disrupt the whole system.

Similarly, C.T. Conover (1984: 288), who was the Comptroller of the Currency at the time of the Continental Illinois National Bank failure in 1984, testified in Congress at the time that

> had Continental failed and been treated in a way in which depositors and creditors were not made whole, we could very well have seen a national, if not an international, financial crisis, the dimensions of which were difficult to imagine. None of us wanted to find out.

Moreover, in 1993, nearly 10 years after the failure of the Continental Bank, Governor LaWare (1993: 96) was still arguing that the bank's failure would have led to the insolvency of

> several hundred [banks]. . .many large companies and banks, both in the United States and in foreign countries, would have lost large amounts as their. . .claims were not honored. . . .[This might] have created a crisis of confidence. . .[and] would have seriously destabilized the entire banking system.

In fact, as was known at the time, had the Continental been resolved on a timely basis, most likely through sale or merger, the loss would have been no greater than 5 percent of its total assets. This is about the same loss as the FDIC suffered when it finally resolved the institution in the early 1990s, after protecting all depositors and creditors.

LaWare argued this despite the results of a U.S. Congressional study (1984) which estimated that if Continental's loss had been as large as 60 cents on the dollar, more than 10 times either the estimated or actual loss, only 27 of the 2,299 banks with exposures to the Continental would have suffered uninsured losses in excess of their capital and become insolvent. These losses would have totaled only $137 million. Another 56 banks would have suffered losses equal to between 50 and 100 percent of their capital in an amount totaling $237 million. If Continental's losses were 10 cents on the dollar, twice the actual amount, not one bank would have suffered losses greater than its capital and only two banks would

The best protection against widespread bank failures and systemic risk is macroeconomic policies that achieve stability and avoid price bubbles that leave banks highly vulnerable to failure. But since the success of such policies is highly questionable, backup prudential policy is desirable. This paper argues that it is possible to reduce both the likelihood and costs of future bank failures as well as any resulting systemic problems without suffering the undesirable side-effects of moral hazard and agency problems that plague many prudential policies. This result can be achieved by introducing an effective system of structured early intervention and resolution (SEIR)—a system that is both incentive compatible and market oriented. Under SEIR, bank failures would be reduced but not eliminated, so that inefficient institutions can exit the industry.

The key feature of the SEIR scheme is an explicit and enforced "closure rule" that resolves banks before their own capital is fully depleted and thereby effectively restricts losses only to shareholders. Explicit full deposit insurance is provided for smaller accounts to prevent systemic risk, but becomes effectively redundant. Because uninsured depositors suffer only small if any losses in bank insolvencies, the major transmission process of systemic risk is not activated and failures of individual banks will not spill over to others. Bank runs, even on individual banks, are far less likely than in a system without a closure rule.

A system of SEIR, although in weakened form, has been included in the United States in the prompt corrective action and least-cost resolution provisions of FDICIA of 1991. Whether it will prevent repeats of the bank failures of the and 1980s, for the same degree of macroeconomic instability, depends on the ability and will of the regulators to enforce the intent of those provisions.

References

Angelini, P.; Mariesca, G.; and Russo, D. (1996) "Systemic Risk in the Netting System." *Journal of Banking and Finance* 20: 853–68.

Baer, H., et al. (1991) Four articles on the U.S. and Swiss clearing systems. In G.G. Kaufman (ed.) *Research in Financial Services* 3: 1–156. Greenwich: JAI Press.

Baer, H., and Klingebiel, D. (1995) "Systemic Risk When Depositors Bear Losses." In G.G. Kaufman (ed.) *Research in Financial Services* 7: 195–302. Greenwich: JAI Press.

---

have suffered losses between 50 and 100 percent of their capital, for a total loss of only $1 million. Systemic risk does not appear to have been a very likely outcome. LaWare's statement represents more "scare talk" and bluster than fact and objective analysis.

Bank for International Settlements (1994) *Annual Report, 1993–1994*. Basle, Switzerland, June.

Bartholomew, P., and Whalen, G. (1995) "Fundamentals of Systemic Risk." In G.G. Kaufman (ed.) *Research in Financial Services* 7: 3–18. Greenwich: JAI Press.

Benston, G. (1994) "International Harmonization of Banking Regulations." *Journal of Financial Services Research* 8: 205–25.

Benston, G.; Brumbaugh, Jr., D.; Guttentag, J.; Herring, R.; Kaufman, G.; Litan, R., and Scott, K. (1989) *Blueprint for Restructuring America's Financial Institutions*. Washington, D.C.: The Brookings Institution.

Benston, G.; Eisenbeis, R.; Horvitz, P.; Kane, E., and Kaufman, G. (1986) *Perspectives on Safe and Sound Banking*. Cambridge: MIT Press.

Benston, G., and Kaufman, G. (1988) *Risk and Solvency Regulation of Depository Institutions: Past Policies and Current Options*. New York: Salomon Brothers Center, Graduate School of Business, New York University.

Benston, G., and Kaufman, G. (1994a) "The Intellectual History of the Federal Deposit Insurance Corporation Improvement Act of 1991. In G. G. Kaufman (ed.) *Reforming Financial Institutions and Markets in the United States*:1–17. Boston: Kluwer.

Benston, G., and Kaufman, G. (1994b) "Improving the FDIC Improvement Act." In G. G. Kaufman (ed.) *Reforming Financial Institutions and Markets in the United States*: 99–120. Boston: Kluwer.

Benston, G., and Kaufman, G. (1995) "Is the Banking and Payments System Fragile?" *Journal of Financial Services Research* 9: 209–40.

Benston, G., and Kaufman, G. (1996) "The Appropriate Role of Bank Regulation." *Economic Journal* 106: 688–97.

Black, F. (1995) "Hedging, Speculation, and Systemic Risk." *Journal of Derivatives* 2:6–8.

Brinkmann, E., Horvitz, P., and Huang, Y. (1996) "Forbearance: An Empirical Analysis." *Journal of Financial Services Research* 10: 27–42.

Calomiris, C., and Gorton, G. (1991) "The Origins of Banking Panics." In R.G. Hubbard (ed.) *Financial Markets and Financial Crises*:109–73. Chicago: University of Chicago Press.

Caprio, Jr., G., and Klingebiel, D. (1995) "Dealing with Bank Insolvencies: Cross Country Experience." Working Paper, World Bank.

Carnell, R. (1992) "A Partial Antidote to Perverse Incentives: Implementing the FDIC Improvement Act of 1991." *Rebuilding Public Confidence Through Financial Reform*: 31–51. Columbus: College of Business, Ohio State University.

Carr, J., Mathewson, F., and Quigley, N. (1995) "Stability in the Absence of Deposit Insurance: The Canadian Banking System, 1890–1966." *Journal of Money, Credit and Banking* 27: 1137–58.

Conover, C.T. (1984). "Testimony." *Inquiry Into the Continental Illinois Corp. and Continental Illinois National Bank: Hearing Before the Subcommittee on Financial Institutions Supervision, Regulation, and Insurance of the Committee on Banking, Finance and Urban Affairs*, 98–111. U.S. House of Representatives, 98th Cong., 2nd Session, 18–19 September and 4 October.

Corrigan, G. (1991) "The Banking-Commerce Controversy Revisited." *Quarterly Review* (Federal Reserve Bank of New York) 16: 1–13.

Davis, E.P. (1992) *Debt, Financial Fragility and Systemic Risk*. Oxford: Oxford University Press.

DeAngelo, H., and DeAngelo, L. (1990) "Dividend Policy and Financial Distress." *Journal of Finance* 45: 1415–31.

Dimson, E., and Marsh, P. (1995) "Capital Requirements for Securities Firms." *Journal of Finance* 50: 821–51.

Eisenbeis, R. (1995) "Private Sector Solutions to Payment System Fragility." *Journal of Financial Services Research* 9: 327–50.

Erdman, P. (1996) "The Day the Check Wasn't in the Mail." *Washington Post National Weekly Edition* : 24–35.

Federal Deposit Insurance Corporation (1995) *1994 Annual Report*, Washington, D.C.

Flannery, M. (1988) "Payments System Risk and Public Policy." In W.S. Haraf and R.M. Kushmeider (eds.) *Restructuring Banking and Financial Services in America*: 261–87. Washington, D.C.: American Enterprise Institute.

Flannery, M. (1995) "Prudential Regulation for Banks." In K. Sawamoto, Z. Nakajima, and H. Taguchi (eds.) *Financial Stability in a Changing Environment*: 281–318. New York: St. Martin's Press.

Follet, K. (1994) *A Dangerous Fortune*. New York: Dell Publishing.

Fox, J. (1995) "Banks Say Too Much Capital Required by Market Risk Rules." *American Banker*, 22 September: 3.

Friedman, M., and Schwartz, A. (1963) *A Monetary History of the United States, 1867–1960*. Princeton: Princeton University Press.

Garcia, G. (1995) "Comparing and Confronting Recent Banking Problems in Foreign Countries." Working Paper, International Monetary Fund.

Gawith, P. (1996) "Bankers Clash Clearing Plan Over Global." *Financial Times*, 27 March: 5.

Goodhart, C.A.E. (1995) *The Central Bank and the Financial System*. Cambridge: MIT Press.

Graham, F. and Horner, J. (1988) "Bank Failure: An Evaluation of the Factors Contributing to the Failure of National Banks." *Proceedings of a Conference on Bank Structure and Competition*: 406–35. Chicago: Federal Reserve Bank of Chicago.

Graham, G. (1996a) "Timing System Set To Take Risk Out Of Settlement." *Financial Times*, 22 April: 6.

Graham, G. (1996b) "Forex Dealers Move to Limit Settlement Risk." *Financial Times*, 5 June: 5.

Greenspan, A. (1995) "Remarks at a Conference on Risk Measurement and Systemic Risk." Washington, D.C.: Board of Governors of the Federal Reserve System.

Humphrey, D. (1987) "Payments System Risk, Market Failure, and Public Policy." In E. Solomon (ed.) *Electronic Funds Transfers and Payments*: 83–110.. Boston: Kluwer Academic Publishers.

Juncker, G., Summers, B., and Young, F. (1991) "A Primer on the Settlement of Payments in the United States." *Federal Reserve Bulletin* 77: 847–58.

Kane, E. (1985) *The Gathering Crises in Federal Deposit Insurance*. Cambridge: MIT Press.

Kane, E. (1989) *The S&L Mess*. Washington, D.C.: Urban Institute.

Kane, E. (1992) "How Incentive-Incompatible Deposit Insurance Plans Fail." In G.G. Kaufman (ed.) *Research in Financial Services* 4: 51–92. Greenwich: JAI Press.

Kane, E. (1995a) "Three Paradigms for the Role of Capitalization Requirements in Insured Financial Institutions." *Journal of Banking and Finance* 19: 431–59.

Kane, E. (1995b) "Why and How Should Depository Institutions Be Regulated." Prepared for conference at Koc University (Turkey).

Kaufman, G. (1988) "Bank Runs: Causes, Benefits and Costs." *Cato Journal* 7: 559–88.

Kaufman, G. (1992) "Capital in Banking: Past, Present and Future." *Journal of Financial Services Research* 5: 385–402.

Kaufman, G. (1994) "Bank Contagion: A Review of the Theory and Evidence." *Journal of Financial Services Research* 8: 123–50.

Kaufman, G. (1995a) "The U.S. Banking Debacle of the 1980s: An Overview and Lessons." *Financier*: 2 9–26.

Kaufman, G. (1995b) "Comment on Systemic Risk." In G.G. Kaufman (ed.) *Research in Financial Services* 7: 47–52. Greenwich: JAI Press.

Kaufman, G. (1996) "Bank Fragility: Perception and Historical Evidence." Chicago: Loyola University Working Paper No. 96-6.

Kaufman, G. (1997, forthcoming) "Lessons for Traditional and Developing Economies from U.S. Deposit Insurance Reform." In G. M. von Furstenberg (ed.) *Global Standards and National Policies: Banking and Finance Regulations in the NAFTA Countries*. Boston: Kluwer Academic Publishers.

Krugman, P. (1994) *Peddling Prosperity*. New York: W.W. Norton.

Kuttner, R. (1991) "Deposit Insurance—Now More Than Ever." *Washington Post National Weekly Edition*: 29.

Lang, L., and Stulz, R. (1992) "Contagion and Competitive Inter-Industry Effects of Bankruptcy Announcements." *Journal of Financial Economics* 32: 45–60.

LaWare, J. (1991) "Testimony." *Economic Implications of the "Too Big to Fail" Policy: Hearing Before the Subcommittee on Economic Stabilization of the Committee on Banking, Finance and Urban Affairs*. U.S. House of Representatives, 102nd Cong., 1st Sess., 9 May.

LaWare J. (1993) "Bank Failures in a Sound Economy." In F. Shadrack and L. Korobon (eds.) *The Basic Elements of Bank Supervision*: 93–100. New York: Federal Reserve Bank of New York.

Mengle, D. (1995) "Regulatory Solutions to Payment System Risk." *Journal of Financial Services Research* 9: 381–92.

Merton R. (1995) "A Functional Perspective of Financial Intermediation." *Financial Management* 24: 23–41.

Mishkin, F. (1991) "Asymmetric Information and Financial Crises." In R.G. Hubbard (ed.) *Financial Markets and Financial Crises*, 69–108. Chicago: University of Chicago Press.

Nakajima, Z., and Taguchi, H. (1995) "Toward a More Stable Financial Framework: An Overview of Recent Bank Disruption Worldwide." In K.

Sawamoto, Z. Nakajima, and H. Taguchi (eds.) *Financial Stability in a Changing Environment*: 41–98. New York: St. Martin's Press.

O'Conner, J.F.T. (1938) *Banking Crisis and Recovery Under the Roosevelt Administration*. Chicago: Callaghan and Co.

Parry, R. (1996) "Global Payments in the 21st Century: A Central Banker's View." *FRBSF Economic Letter*, Federal Reserve Bank of San Francisco, 3 May.

Richards, H. (1995) "Daylight Overdraft Fees and the Federal Reserve's Payment System Risk Policy." *Federal Reserve Bulletin* 81: 1065–77.

Samuelson, R. (1995) "Daiwa's Deeper Lesson." *Washington Post National Weekly Edition*: 5.

Schwartz, A. (1988) "Financial Stability and the Federal Safety Net." In W. Haraf and R.M. Kushmeider (eds.) *Restructuring Banking and Financial Services in America*: 19–30. Washington, D.C.: American Enterprise Institute.

Schwartz, A. (1995). "Systemic Risk and the Macroeconomy." In G.G. Kaufman (ed.) *Research in Financial Services* 7: 19–30. Greenwich: JAI Press.

Selgin, G. (1989) "Legal Restrictions, Financial Weakening, and the Lender of Last Resort." *Cato Journal* 9: 429–59.

Selgin, G. (1992) "Bank Lending 'Manias' in Theory and History." *Journal of Financial Services Research* 5: 169–86.

Shadow Financial Regulatory Committee (1992) "Statement No. 41: An Outline of a Program for Deposit Insurance and Regulatory Reform." *Journal of Financial Services Research* (supplement) 6: S78–S82.

Summers, B., ed. (1994) *The Payment System: Design, Management and Supervision*. Washington, D.C.: International Monetary Fund.

U.S. Congress, House of Representatives, Subcommittee on Financial Institutions Supervision, Regulation and Insurance (1984) *Hearing: Inquiry Into Continental Illinois Corp. and Continental Illinois National Bank*, 98–111. 98th Cong., 2nd Sess., 18–19 September and 4 October.

Williams, M. (1995) "The Efficacy of Accounting-Based Bank Regulation: The Case of the Basle Accord." Working Paper No. 95-5. Santa Monica: Milken Institute.

Bibliography

Aharony, J., and I. Swary. "Contagion Effects of Bank Failures: Evidence from Capital Markets." *Journal of Business* 56 (July 1983): 305–322.

Aharony, J., and I. Swary. "Additional Evidence on the Information-based Contagion Effects of Bank Failures." *Journal of Banking & Finance* 20 (January 1996): 57–69.

Anason, Dean. "Pare 'Too Big to Fail Policy' Minneapolis Fed Chief Suggests." *American Banker*, September 2, 1997, 2.

Andrews, Edmund L. "Japan Catches Up in Bank Failures." *New York Times*, September 10, 1995, E3.

Ange, Jean-Paul, and Jean-Francois Carreras. "Investment Patterns and Practices." In *Transformations in French Business: Political, Economic, and Cultural Changes from 1981 to 1987*, Judith Frommer and Janice McCormick, eds. Westport, CT: Quorum Books, 1989, 50–55.

"Bank Check." *Financial Times*, March 14, 1997, 15.

Bank for International Settlements. *64th Annual Report, 1994*. Basle, Switzerland, June 1994.

"Banking's Biggest Disaster." *The Economist*, July 5, 1997, 69–71.

Banks under Stress. Paris: Organisation for Economic Co-Operation and Development, 1992.

Bardacke, Ted. "Thailand Set to Take on Companies' Bad Debts." *Financial Times*, March 11, 1997, 4.

Bardacke, Ted. "Thai Property Prices Feel the Draught." *Financial Times*, March 12, 1997, 4.

"Barings Failure Will Test Central Bank Cooperation." *International Bank Regulator*, no. 95–10, March 13, 1995, 1, 3.

Barth, James R. *The Great Savings and Loan Debacle*, Washington, DC: American Enterprise Institute Press, 1991.

Bartholomew, Philip F., and Gary W. Whalen. "Analysis of Bank Failure Data: Commercial Bank Resolutions 1980–1994." Paper presented at the Annual Meeting of the Eastern Finance Association, Hilton Head, SC, April 28, 1995a.

Bartholomew, Philip F., and Gary W. Whalen. "Fundamentals of Systemic Risk." In *Research in Financial Services Private and Public Policy*, Vol. 7, George Kaufman, ed. Greenwich, CT: JAI Press, 1995b, 3–17.

Basing, Malcolm P. "Comments on Systemic Risk." In Proceedings, Annual Conference on Bank Structure and Competition, Federal Reserve Bank of Chicago, May 1993, 48–51.

Basle Committee on Banking Supervision. *Core Principles for Effective Banking Supervision*. Basle, Switzerland: Bank of International Settlements, April 1997.

Basle Committee on Banking Supervision. "Report to the Governors on Supervision of Banks' Foreign Establishments," 1975.

Becker, Gary S. "A Theory of Competition among Pressure Groups for Political Influence." *Quarterly Journal of Economics*, August 1983, 371–400.

Bellanger, Serge, and Olivier Blanchard. "Economic Policy." In *Transformations in French Business: Political, Economic, and Cultural Changes from 1981 to 1987*, Judith Frommer and Janice McCormick, eds. Westport, CT: Quorum Books, 1989, 35–49.

Benston, George J. "Federal Regulation of Banking: Historical Overview." In *Deregulating Financial Services: Public Policy in Flux*, George G. Kaufman and Roger C. Kormendi, eds. Cambridge, MA: Ballinger Publishing Co., 1986, 1–47.

Benston, George J. *The Separation of Commercial and Investment Banking*. New York: Oxford University Press, 1990.

Benston, George J. and George G. Kaufman. "The Appropriate Role of Bank Regulation." *The Economic Journal* 106 (May 1996):688–697.

Berger, Allen N., Richard J. Herring, and Giorgio P. Szego. "The Role of Capital in Financial Institutions." *Journal of Banking and Finance* 19 (1995):393–440.

Bernanke, Ben S. "Nonmonetary Effects of the Financial Crises in the Propagation of the Great Depression." *American Economic Review* 73 (June 1983):257–275.

Bernanke, Ben S., and Allen Blinder. "The Federal Funds Rate and Channels of Monetary Transmission." *American Economic Review* 82 (September 1992):901–921.

Betts, Paul. "Italian Savings Bank Looks for Alliance." *Financial Times*, February 12, 1997, 1.

Bhalla, A. S. "Collapse of Barings Bank, Case of Market Failure." *Economic and Political Weekly*, April 1, 1995, 658–662.

Blustein, Paul. "Prelate's Problems: How the Vatican Bank Got Itself Implicated in Ambrosiano Scandal." *Wall Street Journal*, November 23, 1982, 1, 22.

Borio, Claudio E. V. *Leverage and Financing of Non-Financial Companies: An International Perspective*. Basle, Switzerland: Bank for International Settlements, BIS Economic Papers no. 27, May 1990.

Borio, Claudio E. V. *Monetary Policy Operating Procedures in Industrial Countries*. Basle, Switzerland: Bank for International Settlements, BIS Working Papers no. 40, March 1997.

Borio, Claudio E. V., and P. Ven den Bergh. *The Nature and Management of Payment System Risk: An International Perspective*. Basle, Switzerland: Bank for International Settlements, BIS Economic Papers no. 36, February 1993.

Branch, Ben, and Hugh Ray. "The First Republic Case: A Mosaic of Agreements." Presented at the Eastern Finance Association Meeting, Panama City, FL, April 17, 1997.

Brinhammer, H. H. *Money, Banking, and the Canadian Financial System*. Scarborough, Ontario, Canada: Nelson Canada, 1988.

Buchan, David, and Andrew Jack. "More Skeletons in the Closet." *The Financial Times Limited*, September 29, 1994, 19.

Buckley, Neil. "Fraud Costs Belgian Bank $100m." *Financial Times*, March 16, 1997, 24.

Building Better Banks: The Case for Performance-Based Regulation. Chicago: Bank Administration Institute, McKinsey & Co. 1996.

The Burden of Bank Regulation: Tracing the Costs Imposed by Bank Regulation on the American Public. Prepared for the American Bankers Association. Washington, DC: Secura Group, November 16, 1992.

Burton, John. "Seoul to Support Banks with $7bn." *Financial Times*, January 29, 1997, 1.

Burton, John. "S. Korean Steel Group Fails." *Financial Times*, March 20, 1997, 1.

Calomiris, Charles W., and Gary Gorton. "The Origins of Banking Panics." In *Financial Markets and Financial Crises*, R. Glenn Hubbard, ed. Chicago: University of Chicago Press, 1991, 109–173.

Caprio, Gerald, Jr., and Daniela Klingebiel. "Bank Insolvency: Bad Luck, Bad Policy, or Bad Banking?" Unpublished paper. Washington, DC: The World Bank Annual Conference on Development Economics, April 25–26, 1996a.

Caprio, Gerald, Jr., and Daniela Klingebiel. "Bank Insolvencies: Cross-country Experience." Washington, DC: The World Bank, Policy Research Working Paper 1620, July 1996b.

Carrington, Tim. "U.S. Won't Let 11 Largest Banks in Nation Fail." *Wall Street Journal*, September 20, 1984.

CDIC Annual Report 1993. Ottawa, Ontario, Canada: Canada Deposit Insurance Corporation, June 1994.

CDIC Annual Report 1994–1995, Ottawa, Ontario, Canada: Canada Deposit Insurance Corporation, June 1995.

Colby, Laura. "Italian Imbroglio: Vatican Bank Played a Central Role in Fall of Banco Ambrosiano." *Wall Street Journal*, April 27, 1987, 1, 16.

Commission Bankcaire, France. *Annual Report, 1994*.

"Commission Decision of 26 July 1995 Giving Conditional Approval to Aid Granted by France to the Bank Credit Lyonnais." *Official Journal of the European Communities* (English edition), December 21, 1995.

"Competition Policy—France Okays NEC 4.7% Stake in State-Owned Bull." *The Economist Intelligence Unit Ltd.*, EIU Business Europe, July 19, 1991.

Connolly, Walter J. Testimony before the Committee on Banking, Finance, and Urban Affairs, U. S. House, 102nd Cong., 1st Sess. "The Failure of the Bank of New England Corporation and Its Affiliate Banks." Hearing, Serial No. 102–49. June 13, 1991.

Cooke, Stephanie. "Nods, Winks and Subsidies; Single European Market. *Management Today*, March 1993.

"Coping with the Ups and Downs." International Banking Survey. *The Economist*, April 27, 1997, 3–38.

Corcoran, Andrea. "Developing Financial and Operational Performance Standards for Exchange Markets: A Modest Proposal for an International Dialogue." In symposium on "Risk Reduction in Payments, Clearance and Settlement Systems." Goldman, Sachs and Co., New York, January 25 and 26, 1996, 123–132.

Cornford, Andrew, and Jan Kregel. "Globalisation, Capital Flows and

International Regulation." Working Paper no. 161. New York: Jerome Levy Economics Institute of Bard College, May 1996.

Corrigan, E. Gerald. "Payments, Clearance and Settlement Systems: The Systemic Risk Connection." In symposium on "Risk Reduction in Payments, Clearance and Settlement Systems." Goldman, Sachs and Co., New York, January 25 and 26, 1996, 13–18.

"Credit Immobilier Warns on CFF bid." *Financial Times*, February 14, 1997, 14.

Dale, Richard. *International Banking Deregulation*. Cambridge, MA: Blackwell Publishers, 1992.

Davis, E. Philip. *Debt, Financial Fragility, and Systemic Risk*, revised and expanded edition. New York: Oxford University Press, 1995.

Dawkins, William. "Japanese Lender Struggles for Survival." *Financial Times*, February 3, 1997, 21.

Dawkins, William. "Tokyo Package Aims to Spur Property Market." *Financial Times*, April 1, 1997, 1.

Dawkins, William. "Japan Banks Merger Ahead of 'Big Bang.'" *Financial Times*, April 2, 1997, 21.

Dawkins, William, and Gwen Robinson. "New Shake-up for Japanese Banks." *Financial Times*, April 2, 1997, 1.

"Debit Lyonnais's Encore." *The Economist*, March 25, 1995, 18–20.

Demirguc-Kunt, Asli, and Enrica Detragiache. "The Determinants of Banking Crises: Evidence from Developed and Developing Countries." World Bank and IMF, unpublished paper, July 1997.

Diamond, Douglas W., and Philip H. Dybvig. "Bank Runs, Deposit Insurance, and Liquidity." *Journal of Political Economy* 91 (June 1983):401–419.

DiLorenzo, Thomas J. "The Political Economy of National Industrial Policy." *Cato Journal* 4, no. 2 (Fall 1984):587–607.

DuBois, Martin. "Scandal Imperils Antwerp Diamond Hub." *Wall Street Journal*, July 3, 1997, A8.

Edwards, Franklin R. "The Future Financial Structure: Fears and Policies." In *Restructuring Banking and Financial Services in America*, William S. Haraf and Rose Marie Kushmeider, eds. Washington, DC: American Enterprise Institute, 1988, 113–155.

Eisenbeis, Robert A. "Risk as a Criterion for Expanding Banking Activities." In *Deregulating Financial Services: Public Policy in Flux*, George G. Kaufman and Roger C. Kormendi, eds. Cambridge, MA: Ballinger Publishing Co., 1986, 169–189.

Eisenbeis, Robert A. "Systemic Risk: Bank Deposits and Credit." In *Research in Financial Services Private and Public Policy*, Vol. 7, George Kaufman, ed. Greenwich, CT: JAI Press, 1995, 55–86.

Elliot, Harvey. "Air France Climbdown Angers UK Carriers." *Times*, October 26, 1993.

Ely, Bert, and Vicki Vanderhoff. *The Farm Credit System: Reckless Lender to Rural America*. Prepared for the American Bankers Association. Alexandria, VA: Ely and Co., November 1990.

Esty, Benjamin C. "Liability Rules and Risk Taking in Commercial Banks." Unpublished manuscript, Harvard Business School, September 9, 1996.

Failed Bank Cost Analysis: 1985–1990. Washington, DC: FDIC, Division of Accounting and Corporate Services Financial Reporting Branch, 1991.

"For FDIC, Bolstering the Economy Was Key." *American Banker*, January 8, 1991, 1.

Federal Reserve Bank of Cleveland, Annual Report 1985. Federal Reserve Bank of Cleveland, 1986.

FitzGerald, E. V. K. "Intervention versus Regulation: The Role of the IMF in Crisis Prevention and Management." Working Paper no. 160. New York: Jerome Levy Economics Institute of Bard College, May 1966.

Flemming, Charles. "American Express and Credit Lyonnais May Be Close to Pact for Issuing Credit Cards." *Wall Street Journal*, February 21, 1997.

Folkerts-Landau, David, Takatoshi Ito, et al. *International Capital Markets: Developments, Prospects, and Policy Issues*. Washington, DC: International Monetary Fund, August 1995.

"France: Former Bull Chief Slams Government for Mismanagement of the Company." Reuter Textline Computergram, February 6, 1991.

Frankel, Allen B., and David E. Palmer. "The Management of Financial Risks at German Nonfinancial Firms: The Case of Metallgesellschaft." Washington, DC: Board of Governors of the Federal Reserve System, International Finance Discussion Papers, no. 560, August 1996.

Franks, Julian R., Kjell G. Nyborg, and Walter N. Torous. "A Comparison of US, UK, and German Insolvency Codes." *Financial Management* 25, no. 3 (Autumn 1996):86–101.

Fraser, Donald D., and R. Malcolm Richards. "The Penn Square Bank Failure and Inefficient Market." *Journal of Portfolio Management*, Spring 1985, 34–36.

"French Banks: The Cracks Show." *The Economist*, May 4, 1996, 74–75.

Friedman, Milton, and Anna J. Schwartz. *A Monetary History of the United States, 1867–1960*. Princeton, NJ: Princeton University Press, 1963.

Friedman, Milton, and Anna J. Schwartz. *The Great Contraction 1929–1933*. Princeton, NJ: Princeton University Press, 1965.

Garcia, Gillian. "Regulatory Theory and Regulatory Reform: A Comment on 'The Financial Institutions Reform, Recovery, and Enforcement Act." In *Research In International Business: Emerging Challenges for the International Financial Services Industry*, Vol. 9, James R. Barth and Philip Bartholomew, eds. Greenwich, CT: JAI Press, 1992, 107–116.

Gargan, Edward A. "Singapore Defends Itself over Barings." *New York Times*, March 2, 1995, D1, D6.

Garten, Helen A. *Why Bank Regulation Failed: Designing a Bank Regulatory Strategy for the 1990s*. Westport, CT: Quorum Books, 1991.

Garten, Helen A. "Political Analysis of Bank Failure Resolution." *Boston University Law Review* 74, no. 3 (May 1994): 429–479.

Gerlach, S., and F. Smets. "Contagious Speculative Attacks." Basle, Switzerland, Bank for International Settlements, Working Paper No. 23, September 1994.

Gilbert, R. Alton. "A Re-examination of the History of Bank Failures, Contagion, and Banking Panics." *Proceedings of a Conference on Bank Structure and Competition*, May 11–13, 1988, Federal Reserve Bank of Chicago, 128–152.

Gilbert, R. Alton, and Geoffrey E. Wood. "Coping with Bank Failures: Some Lessons from the United States and the United Kingdom." *Review*, Federal Reserve Bank of St. Louis, December 1986, 5–14.

Glain, Steve, and Norihiko Shirouzu. "Japan's Financial Crisis Reaches Insurers." *Wall Street Journal*, April 28, 1997, A 15.

Goldstein, Morris, and Phillip Turner. *Banking Crises in Emerging Economies: Origins and Policy Options*. Basle, Switzerland: Bank for International Settlements, BIS Economic Papers no. 46, October 1996.

Goodfriend, Marvin, and Robert G. King. "Financial Deregulation, Monetary Policy, and Central Banking. In *Restructuring Banking and Financial Services in America*, William S. Haraf and Rose Marie Kushmeider, eds. Washington, DC: American Enterprise Institute, 1988, 216–253.

Goodhart, C. A. E. *The Central Bank and the Financial System*. Cambridge, MA: MIT Press, 1995.

Goodhart, Charles A. E., Phillipp Hartman, David T. Llewellyn, Liliana Rojas-Suarez, and Steven R. Weisbrod. *Financial Regulation: Why, How and Where Now?* England, Monograph for the Central Bank Governors' Meeting at the Bank of England, June 6, 1997 (Preliminary).

Gordon, Patrice L., and Thomas Lutton. *The Changing Business of Banking: A Study of Failed Banks from 1987–1992.* Washington, DC: Congressional Budget Office, 1994.

Gorton, Gary. "Clearinghouses and the Origins of Central Banking in the United States." *Journal of Economic History,* June 1985, 277–283.

Gorton, Gary. "Bank Panics and Business Cycles." *Oxford Economic Papers,* December 1988, 751–781.

Graham, George. "Bankers Weigh Loss." *Financial Times,* April 4, 1997.

Graham, Robert. "Treasury Urged to Buy Bank of Italy." *Financial Times,* February 12, 1997, 3.

Graham, Robert. "Calvi Death Arrest Sought." *Financial Times,* April 10, 1997, 2.

Greenspan, Alan. "FDICIA and the Future of Banking Law and Regulation." Proceedings, Annual Conference on Bank Structure and Competition, Federal Reserve Bank of Chicago, May 1993, 1–8.

Greenspan, Alan, Chairman, Board of Governors of the Federal Reserve System. Statement before the Committee on Banking, Housing, and Urban Affairs, U.S. Senate, November 27, 1995.

Greenspan, Alan, Chairman, Board of Governors of the Federal Reserve System. Testimony before the Subcommittee on Capital Markets, Securities and Government-Sponsored Enterprises of the Committee on Banking and Financial Services, U.S. House of Representatives, March 19, 1997a.

Greenspan, Alan. Remarks at the Annual Conference of the Association of Private Enterprise Education, Arlington, Va, April 12, 1997b.

Greenspan, Alan. Remarks by the Chairman at the annual meeting and conference of the Conference of State Bank Supervisors, San Diego, California, May 3, 1997.

Gup, Benton E. *Targeting Fraud: Uncovering and Deterring Fraud in Financial Institutions.* Burr Ridge, IL: Irwin Professional Publishing, 1995.

Hanc, George. "History of the Eighties, Lessons for the Future: A Summary of the Findings." Washington, DC: FDIC, December 16, 1996.

Hansell, Saul. "A U.S. Look for Lessons in Barings." *New York Times,* March 6, 1995, D1.

Haugen, Robert A., and Lemma W. Senbet. "The Insignificance of Bankruptcy Costs to the Theory of Optimal Capital Structure." *Journal of Finance,* May 1978, 383–393.

Helfer, Ricki, Chairman, FDIC. Remarks before the Bank Administration Institute, Washington, DC, December 11, 1996.

Hoenig, Thomas M. "Bank Regulation: Asking the Right Questions."
    Federal Reserve Bank of Kansas City, *Economic Review* (First
    Quarter 1997):5–10.

Honohan, Patrick. *Banking System Failures in Developing and Tran-
    sition Countries: Diagnosis and Prediction*. Working Paper no.
    39. Basle: Bank for International Settlements, January 1997.

Hutton, Bethan, and Jonathan Annells. "Property Blues Show Sign of
    Lifting." *Financial Times*, April 2, 1997, 7.

Ingves, Stefan, and Goran Lind. "The Management of the Bank Cri-
    sis—In Retrospect." *Sveriges Riksbank, Quarterly Review*, Jan-
    uary 1996, 5–18.

Irvine, Steven, and David Shirreff. "Why Barings Was Doomed." *Eu-
    romoney*, March 1995, 38–41.

Jack, Andrew. "Credit Lyonnais Sells Swedish Unit." *Financial Times*,
    February 19, 1997a, 16.

Jack, Andrew. "France Ready to Pay $3.5bn for GAN Rescue Package."
    Financial Times, February 22, 1997b, 1.

Jack, Andrew. "Banque Hervet May Be Offered for Public Sale." *Fi-
    nancial Times*, March 3, 1997c, 21.

Jack, Andrew. "Taxpayers Foot Bill for GAN's Mistakes." *Financial
    Times*, March 5, 1997d, 16.

Jack, Andrew. "Credit Lyonnais Reports FFr202 Profit." *Financial
    Times*, March 21, 1997e, 19.

Jack, Andrew. "Credit Lyonnais Boss Defiant." *Financial Times*, March
    24, 1997f, 19.

Jack, Andrew. "Market Sees Suez-Lyonnaise Merger Soon." *Financial
    Times*, March 25, 1997g, 16.

Jack, Andrew, and John Murray Brown. "Credit Lyonnais Plans Stake
    Sale." *Financial Times*, March 14, 1997, 17.

Jack, Andrew, and Emma Tucker. "Credit Lyonnais Plans Sell-off
    Strategy." *Financial Times Limited*, January 8, 1997a, 3.

Jack, Andrew, and Emma Tucker. "France Plans Extra $5bn for Bank."
    Financial Times, February 21, 1997b, 1.

Jackson, William. "Universal Banking (Deposits and Diversified In-
    dustries) in One Company?" Washington, DC: Congressional Re-
    search Report, 95–579E, April 25, 1995.

James, Christopher. "The Losses Realized in Bank Failures." *Journal
    of Finance* 46, no. 4 (September 1991):1223–1242.

"Japan Suffers Eighth Bank Failure of the Year." *New York Times*,
    December 8, 1995, D4.

"Japan's Banks Near Danger Zone as 'Big Bang' Looms." *Financial
    Times*, January 28, 1997, 23.

"Japanese Banks: Rot." *The Economist*, April 5, 1997, 69.

Jayanti, S. V., Ann Marie Whyte, and A. Quang Do. "Bank Failures

and Contagion Effects: Evidence from Britain and Canada."
Journal of Economics and Business 48, no. 2 (May 1996):103–
116.

Jefferson, Thomas. Letter to Samuel Kercheval, July 12, 1816. Chamber inscription, Thomas Jefferson Memorial, Washington, DC.

Kaminsky, Graciela L., and Carmen M. Reinhart. "The Twin Crises: The Causes of Banking and Balance-of-Payments Problems." Unpublished paper, Board of Governors of the Federal Reserve System, September 1966.

Kane, Edward J. "How Market Forces Influence the Structure of Financial Regulation." In *Restructuring Banking and Financial Services in America*, William S. Haraf and Rose Marie Kushmeider, eds. Washington, DC: American Enterprise Institute, 1988, 343–382.

Kane, Edward J. *The S&L Insurance Mess: How Did It Happen?* Washington, DC: Urban Institute Press, 1989.

Kane, Edward J. "Dangers of a Bifurcated Banking System." Proceedings, Annual Conference on Bank Structure and Competition, Federal Reserve Bank of Chicago, May 1993.

Kaufman, George G. "Are Some Banks Too Large to Fail? Myth and Reality." *Contemporary Policy Issues* 8, (October 1990):1–14.

Kaufman, George G. "Comment on Systemic Risk." In *Research in Financial Services Private and Public Policy*, Vol. 7, George Kaufman, ed. Greenwich, CT: JAI Press, 1995, 47–52.

Kaufman, George G. "Bank Fragility: Perception and Historical Evidence." Unpublished paper. Loyola University and the Federal Reserve Bank of Chicago, January 27, 1997.

Kindleberger, Charles P. *Manias, Panics and Crashes*. London: Macmillan, 1978; 3rd ed. New York: John Wiley and Sons, 1996.

Knight, Gerry. "Derivatives Dealer Fined $10 Million; Agency Cites 'Fraud' by Bankers Trust Unit." *Washington Post*, December 23, 1994, A1.

Kopcke, Richard W. "Safety and Soundness of Financial Intermediaries: Capital Requirements, Deposit Insurance, and Monetary Policy." *New England Economic Review*, November–December 1995, 37–65.

Kryzanowski, Lawrence, and Gordon S. Roberts. "The Performance of the Canadian Banking System, 1920–1940." In *Proceedings: Conference on Bank Structure and Competition*. May 3–5, 1989. Chicago: Federal Reserve Bank of Chicago, 1989, 221–232.

Kyei, Alexander. "Deposit Protection Arrangements: A Survey." Washington, DC: International Monetary Fund, Working Paper WP/95/135, December 1995.

Lamy, R. E., and G. R. Thompson. "Penn Square: Problem Loans and

Insolvency." *Journal of Financial Research* 9 (Summer 1986): 103–111.

Layne, Richard. "Banks Crack Drexel Collateral Gridlock." *American Banker*, February 26, 1990, 1.

Leeson, Nick, and Edward Whitely. *Rouge Trader: How I Brought Down Barings Bank and Shook the Financial World*. Boston: Little, Brown and Co., 1996.

Lepetit, J. F. "Comment on Lender of Last Resort." In *Financial Crises, Theory, History, and Policy*, C. P. Kindleberger and J.P. Laffargue, eds. Cambridge: Cambridge University Press, 1982.

"The Lesson of Credit Lyonnais." *The Economist*, July 5, 1997, 17.

Lieven, Anatol. "Hungary Covers Bank's Losses." *Financial Times*, April 25, 1997, 2.

Lindgren, Carl-Johan, Gillian Garcia, and Matthew I. Saal. *Bank Soundness and Macroeconomic Policy*. Washington, DC: International Monetary Fund, 1996.

Logue, Dennis E., and Pietra Rivoli. "Some Consequences of Bank's LDC Loans: A Note." *Journal of Financial Services Research* 6. (1992):37–47.

Lohr, Steve. "Troubled Banks and the Role of the Press." *New York Times*, February 18, 1991, 33.

McConnell, Bill. "Chase, Citi Opposing Push for Quick Passage of Financial Reform." *American Banker*, October 6, 1997, 4.

McGee, Suzanne. "Bank of Tokyo Blames Loss on Bad Model." *Wall Street Journal*, March 28, 1997, A3.

McNevin, Ambrose. "France: EC Tackles France over Bull." Reuters Textline, Computing, October 14, 1993.

Macleod, Allison. "The Pope's Fallible Banker." *Euromoney*, October 1982, 56–64.

Madura, Jeff, and Kenneth Bartunek. "Contagion Effects of the Bank of New England's Failure." *Review of Financial Economics* 4, no. 1 (1994):25–37.

Madura, Jeff, and A. L. Tucker. "Information Effects of First Republic Bank's Failure." *Applied Financial Economics*, June 1991, 89–96.

Martin, Neil A. "Japan's Turn." *Barron's*, April 14, 1997, 18–20.

Mason, John. "$1.2bn Swindler's Account Closed." *Financial Times*, April 4, 1997, 8.

Mayer, Martin. "Too Big Not to Fail." *Forbes*, April 5, 1991, 68, 71.

Mayer, Martin. "Don't Bank on Reform." *Wall Street Journal*, March 28, 1997, A16.

Meehan John, and Joe Weber. "Bank Scoreboard: A Year of Shaking Off the Bad Loan Blues." *Business Week*, April 27, 1992, 96, 98–99.

Meltzer, Allen H. "Regulatory Arrangements, Financial Stability and Regulatory Reform." In *Financial Stability in a Changing Environment*, Kuniho Sawamoto, Zenta Nakajima, and Hiroo Taguchi, eds. New York: St. Martin's Press, 1995, 7–25.

Miller, Merton H. "Do the M&M propositions apply to banks?" *Journal of Banking & Finance* 19 (1995):483–489.

Mishkin, Frederic S. "Asymmetric Information and Financial Crises: A Historical Perspective." In *Financial Markets and Financial Crises*, R. Glenn Hubbard, ed. Chicago: University of Chicago Press, 1991, 69–108.

Musumeci, James J., and Joseph F. Sinkey, Jr. "The International Debt Crisis and Bank Security Returns Surrounding Citicorp's Loan-Loss Decision of May 19, 1987." In *Proceedings of a Conference on Bank Structure and Competition*, May 11–13, 1988. Chicago: Federal Reserve Bank of Chicago, 1988, 426–459.

Nagarajan, S., and C.W. Sealey. "Can Delegating Bank Regulation to Market Forces Really Work?" Presented at the Eastern Finance Association Meeting, Panama City, FL, April 17, 1997.

Nanto, Dick K. "Japan's Looming Bank Crises: A Half Trillion Dollars in Non-Performing Loans?" Washington, DC: Library of Congress, CRS Report no.94–667E, August 19, 1994.

Nanto, Dick K. "Japan's Banking Crises: Causes and Probable Effects." Washington, DC: Library of Congress, CRS Report no. 95–1034 E, October 6, 1995a.

Nanto, Dick K. "The Federal Reserve's Arrangement for Emergency Loans to Japanese Banks." Washington, DC: Library of Congress, CRS Report no. 96–19E, December 27, 1995b.

Nanto, Dick K. "Japan's Banking "Crises": Bad Loans, Bankruptcy, and Illegal Activity." Washington, DC: Library of Congress, CRS Report no. 96–837 E, October 11, 1996.

Nanto, Dick K., William D. Jackson, and F. Jean Wells. "The Daiwa Bank Problem: Background and Policy Issues." Washington, DC: Library of Congress, CRS Report no. 95–1164E, December 19, 1995.

Nash, Nathaniel C. "France Offers Plan to Bail Out Credit Lyonnais for $27 Billion." *New York Times*, March 18, 1995, 37–38.

Okina, Yuri. "Resolution Methods for Bank Failure in Japan." *Japan Research Quarterly* 2, no. 3 (Summer 1993):78–88.

Ollard, Will, and Nick Routledge. "How the Bank of England Failed the JMB Test." *Euromoney*, February 1985, 49–56.

Olson, James S. *Saving Capitalism: The Reconstruction Finance Corporation and the New Deal, 1933–1940*, Princeton, NJ: Princeton University Press, 1988.

Osterberg, William P., and James B. Thomson. "Depositor Preference Legislation and Failed Banks' Resolution Costs." Presented at the Eastern Finance Association Meeting, Panama City, FL, April 14, 1997.

Park, Sangkyun. "Bank Failure, Contagion in Historical Perspective." *Journal of Monetary Economics* 28 (1991):271–286.

Peavy, J.W., III and G. H. Hempel. "The Penn Square Bank Failure." *Journal of Banking and Finance* 12 (March 1988):141–150.

Peltzman, Sam. "The Economic Theory of Regulation after a Decade of Deregulation." Washington, DC: Brookings Papers: Microeconomics, 1989.

Phillips, Susan M. governor of the Federal Reserve. Testimony before the Subcommittee on Financial Institutions and Regulatory Relief of the Committee on Banking, Housing, and Urban Affairs, U.S. Senate, March 20, 1997.

Pitt, Harvey L., David M. Miles, Anthony Ain, David B. Hardison, and Susan White Haag, *The Law of Financial Services*, Vol. 1. Englewood Cliffs, NJ: Prentice Hall Law & Business, 1994, 1994 Supplement, Financial and Managerial Resources: Source of Strength Policy, 40.1–40.8.

Plender, John. "Fears of Collateral Damage." *Financial Times*, April 1, 1997, 21.

Prescott, Edward S. "The Pre-Commitment Approach in a Model of Regulatory Banking Capital." Federal Reserve Bank of Richmond, *Economic Quarterly* (Winter 1997):23–50.

Proxmire, William. Opening Statement, Chrysler Corporation Loan Guarantee Act, Hearing before the Committee on Banking, Housing, and Urban Affairs, U.S. Senate, 96th Cong., 2nd Sess., May 20, 1980, 1–4.

Quinn, Brian. "The Role of Supervision and International Coordination." In symposium on "Risk Reduction in Payments, Clearance and Settlement Systems," Goldman, Sachs and Co., New York, January 25 and 26, 1996, 31–36.

Rawsthorn, Alice. "Bank's Rescue Leaves Bitter Taste—The Credit Lyonnais Baleout Is Unpopular." *The Financial Times Limited*, February 10, 1994a, 27.

Rawsthorn, Alice. "Survey of Rhone Alps." *The Financial Times Limited*, March 29, 1994b, 35.

Reich, Robert B., and John B. Donahue. *New Deals, The Chrysler Revival and the American System*. New York: Times Books, 1985.

"Regional Bank, Credit Cooperative Fail on Same Day in Japan." *BNA's Banking Reporter* 65 (September 11, 1995), 411.

"Report of the Presidential Task Force on Market Mechanisms." In

Black Monday and the Future of Financial Markets, R.W. Kamphuis, R.C. Kormendi, and J.W.H. Watson, eds., Homewood, IL: Irwin, 1988.

Resolution Trust Corporation: Open Bank Assistance. Washington, DC: American Bankers Association, Office of Research and Statistics, May 1990.

Righting the Regulatory Balance: Reconstructing a Banking System That Works. Prepared for the American Bankers Association. Washington, DC: Institute for Strategy Development, November 1992.

Roe, Mark J. *Strong Managers, Weak Owners: The Political Roots of American Corporate Finance*. Princeton, NJ: Princeton University Press, 1994.

Robinson, Gwen. "Japanese Bank Chief Set to Quit in Growing Turmoil." *Financial Times*, April 1, 1997, 1.

Ross, Irwin. "Chrysler on the Brink." *Fortune*, February 9, 1981, 38–42.

Sachs, Jeffrey D., Aaron Tornell, and Andres Valasco. "Financial Crises in Emerging Markets: The Lessons from 1995." *Brookings Papers on Economic Activity*, No. 1, 1996, 147–215.

Samson, William D., and Benton E. Gup. "The Hidden Side of Corporate Restructuring." *Tax Analysts-Tax Notes*, November 13, 1989, 877–884.

Sapsford, Jathon. "Japan Vows Support for Large Banks, Suggesting a Slow Start for Big Bang." *Wall Street Journal*, February 11, 1997a, A17.

Sapsford, Jathon. "Japan's Hashimoto Orders New Reforms to Bolster Sluggish Real-Estate Market." *Wall Street Journal*, March 19, 1997b, A15.

Sapsford, Jathon. "Japanese Panel Backs Creation of Real-Estate Investment Trusts." *Wall Street Journal*, April 1, 1997c, A15.

"Sayonara?" *The Economist*, February 15, 1997, 73.

Schuman, Michael. "Kia Seeks Protection from Its Creditors, Raising Toll in Korea's Corporate Crises." *Wall Street Journal*, September 23, 1997, A19.

Schwartz, Anna J. "The Effects of Regulation on Systemic Risk." In *Proceedings of a Conference on Bank Structure and Competition*, May 11–13, 1988. Chicago: Federal Reserve Bank of Chicago, 1988a, 28–34.

Schwartz, Anna J. "Financial Stability and the Federal Safety Net." In *Restructuring Banking and Financial Services in America*, William S. Haraf and Rose Marie Kushmeider, eds. Washington, DC: American Enterprise Institute, 1988b, 34–62.

Schwartz, Anna J. "Systemic Risk and the Macroeconomy." In *Research in Financial Services Private and Public Policy*, Vol. 7, George Kaufman, ed. Greenwich, CT: JAI Press, 1995, 19–30.

Seger, Martha R. "Remarks for the Panel, 'Lessons from October 19, 1987.'" In *Proceedings of a Conference on Bank Structure and Competition*, May 11–13, 1988. Chicago: Federal Reserve Bank of Chicago, 1988, 42–44.

Sesit, Michael R., and Sara Calian. "NatWest Lifts Loss on Options Mispricing to $136 Million, and U.K. Probes Case." *Wall Street Journal*, March 14, 1997, B3A.

Sheng, Andrew. *Bank Restructuring: Lessons from the 1980s*. Washington, DC: The World Bank, 1996.

"A Sorry Way to Sell a State." *The Economist*, January 18, 1997, 72–73.

Statton, Thomas H. "Government-Sponsored Enterprises Also Need Better Supervision." *Financier*, October 1989, 33–36.

Steiner, Robert. "Raging Dollar Threatens Tokyo's Banks." *Wall Street Journal*, February 13, 1997, A12.

Steinmetz, Greg. "Swiss: Miss: Banks Falter, Jobs Are Lost in Lengthy Recession." *Wall Street Journal*, February 24, 1997, A1, A13.

Stern, Gary H. "The Too-Big-to-Fail-Problem." *Wall Street Journal*, October 6, 1997.

Stigler, George J. "The Theory of Economic Regulation." *Bell Journal of Economics and Management Science* 2 (Spring 1971):3–21.

Sugawara, Sandra. "Japan Comes to Aid of Troubled Banks." *Washington Post*, March 29, 1997, F2.

Sundararajan, V., and Tomas J. T. Balino. *Banking Crises: Cases and Issues*. Washington, DC: International Monetary Fund, 1991.

Swary, I. "Stock Market Reaction to Regulatory Action in the Continental Illinois Crisis." *Journal of Business* 59 (July 1986):451–473.

Swoboda, Frank. "American Airlines Pilots Approve 5-Year Contract." *Washington Post*, May 6, 1997, C1, C4.

Swoboda, Frank, and Judith Evans. "Clinton Intervenes to Halt Airline Strike." *Washington Post*, February 15, 1997, A1, A16.

Tallman, Ellis. "Some Unanswered Questions about Bank Panics." Atlanta, GA: Federal Reserve Bank of Atlanta, November–December 1988, 2–21.

"Taxpayers May Foot $19bn Credit Lyonnais Rescue." *The Banker*, October 1996, 5.

Tett, Gillian. "Caretaker Bank Set Up to Manage Hanwa Closure." *Financial Times*, April 10, 1997a, 16.

Tett, Gillian. "Support Grows for Nippon Credit Rescue." *Financial Times*, April 24, 1997b, 20.

Trigaux, Robert. "Regulators Put Drexel on Own in Fast Decision." *American Banker*, February 16, 1990, 1.

Tucker, Emma, and Jack Andrew. "Green Light for Credit Lyonnais Rescue: Commission Imposes Conditions on French Government's Costly Package." *The Financial Times Limited*, July 27, 1997, 2.

Tucker, Emma, and Andrew Fisher. "Unfair Advantage." *Financial Times*, February 4, 1997, 17.

United States Congress. *Findings of the Chrysler Corporation Loan Guarantee Board*. Subcommittee on Economic Stabilization of the Committee on Banking, Finance and Urban Affairs, House of Representatives, 96th Cong., 2nd Sess., May 12, 1980, Department of Treasury News, Fact Sheet, 3–15.

United States Congress. *The Failure of the Bank of New England Corporation and Its Affiliate Banks*. Hearing before the Committee on Banking, Finance and Urban Affairs, U.S. House, 102 Cong., 1st Sess., June 13, 1991, Serial No. 102–49, 1991.

United States Department of Treasury. *Modernizing the Financial System: Recommendations for Safer, More Competitive Banks*. Washington, DC, February 1991.

United States Department of Treasury. *National Treatment Study, 1994*. Washington, DC, December 1994.

United States General Accounting Office. *Bank Supervision: OCC's Supervision of the Bank of New England Was Not Timely or Resourceful*. GAO/GGD-91–128, September 1991a.

United States General Accounting Office. *Deposit Insurance: A Strategy for Reform*. GAO/GGD-91–26, March 1991b.

United States General Accounting Office. *Bank Regulatory Structure: The Federal Republic of Germany*. GAO/GGD-94–134BR, May 1994a.

United States General Accounting Office. *Bank Regulatory Structure: The United Kingdom*. GAO/GGD-95–38, December 1994b.

United States General Accounting Office. *International Banking*. GAO/GGD-94–68, March 1994c.

United States General Accounting Office. *Bank Regulatory Structure: Canada*. GAO/GGD-95–223, September 1995a.

United States General Accounting Office. *Bank Regulatory Structure: France*. GAO/GGD-95–152, August 1995b.

United States General Accounting Office. *Bank Oversight Structure: Canada*. GAO/GGD-97–23, November 1996a.

United States General Accounting Office. *Bank Regulatory Structure: Japan*. GAO/GGD-97–5, December 1996b.

United States General Accounting Office. *Bank Oversight Structure:*

U.S. and Foreign Experience May Offer Lessons for Modernizing U.S. Structure. GAO/GGD-97–23, November 1996c.

Vaubel, Roland. "International Debt, Bank Failures, and the Money Supply: The Thirties and the Eighties." *Cato Journal* 4, no. 1 (Summer 1994):249–267.

Wall, Larry D. "Too-Big-to-Fail, Federal Reserve Bank of Atlanta." *Economic Review*, January–February 1993, 1–14.

Wall, Larry D., and David R. Peterson. "The Effect of Continental Illinois' Failure on the Financial Performance of Other Banks." *Journal of Monetary Economics* 26, no. 1 (August 1990):77–99.

Walsh, Sharon. "How Penalties Become Pay-Back." *Washington Post*, February 2, 1997.

White, Lawrence J. *The S&L Debacle: Public Policy Lessons for Bank and Thrift Regulation*. New York: Oxford University Press, 1991.

White, Michelle J. "The Corporate Bankruptcy Decision." *Journal of Economic Perspectives*, Spring 1989, 129–151.

Wilmarth, Arthur E., Jr. "Too Big to Fail, Too Few to Serve? The Potential Risks of Nationwide Banks." *Iowa Law Review*, 1992, 957–1081.

Wilmarth, Arthur E., Jr. "Too Good to Be True? The Unfulfilled Promises behind Big Bank Mergers." *Stanford Journal of Law, Business & Finance* 2, no. 1 (Fall 1995):1–88.

Yearbook of International Organizations, 1996/1997. Munich, Germany: K.G. Saur Verlag GmbH. and Co., June 1996.

Zang, Peter G. *Barings Bankruptcy and Financial Derivatives*. Singapore: World Scientific Publishing Co. Pte. Ltd., 1995.

Index

About the Author

BENTON E. GUP is Professor in Finance and Chair of Banking at the University of Alabama's College of Commerce, Tuscaloosa. He is known internationally as a lecturer in executive development and as a consultant in finance to government and industry. He is the author or coauthor of several major textbooks in banking, finance, and investment, and his many articles on financial topics have appeared in the major journals of his field.

ISBN 1-56720-208-X

EAN

9 781567 202083

HARDCOVER BAR CODE